the Celebration book

FAMILY LIFE TREASURY BOOK

FUN THINGS TO DO WITH YOUR FAMILY ALL YEAR-ROUND

GEORGIANA WALKER · EDITOR
CHIZUKO YASUDA · ILLUSTRATOR

 A Division of G/L Publications, Glendale, California, U.S.A.

*To the many families
who celebrated good times together...
and wrote about their celebrations.
Their stories make this book possible.*

A celebration is...
joyfully taking time to show that you feel
someone or something is truly important.

Editor's Preface

In the nearly three years that we have been publishing *Family Life Today* we have received many letters from readers telling us how they are using ideas from the magazine....

"We're having fun with the family time ideas. The Family Fun Coupons were great!"

"We'll never forget the evening we had our 'Appreciate Everyone in Your Family' time. I kept the notes we wrote to each other telling why each person is special."

"Please send us another copy of the magazine with the poem 'Children Won't Wait'—we want to share it with some friends."

In fact... it was comments from readers that inspired us to put together some Family Life Treasury books. And that is what *The Celebration Book* is—a treasury of articles and ideas from *Family Life Today* to help families celebrate good times together.

It's been a kind of celebration working on this book. With a pot of paste, stacks of *Family Life Today* magazines and a sharp pair of scissors decorating my desk the fun began. Just one problem. I got so carried away that I ended up with enough celebration ideas for two books! Many of our favorite ideas must be filed away until we do another Family Life Treasury Book.

And so, here it is—*The Celebration Book*—packed full of ideas to help you have good family times...summer and winter...springtime and autumn...as you celebrate your family and your faith.

Georgiana Walker

Contents

Biblical Thoughts on Celebration

• "The Lord makes us strong! Sing praises!... Sing accompanied by drums; pluck the sweet lyre and harp. Sound the trumpet! Come to the joyous celebrations... for God has given us these times of joy."

• "During those celebration days... you must explain to your children why you are celebrating—it is a celebration of what the Lord did for you."

• "The people went away to eat a festive meal and to send presents; it was a time of great and joyful celebration because they could hear and understand God's words."

• "Accept our praise, O Lord, for all your glorious power. We will... celebrate your mighty acts!"

Scriptures are quoted from Psalm 81:1-4; Exodus 13:8; Nehemiah 8:12; Psalm 21:13 in *The Living Bible* paraphrase.

Celebrations—Family Style

Parties That Say "I Love You"

by Marion Duckworth

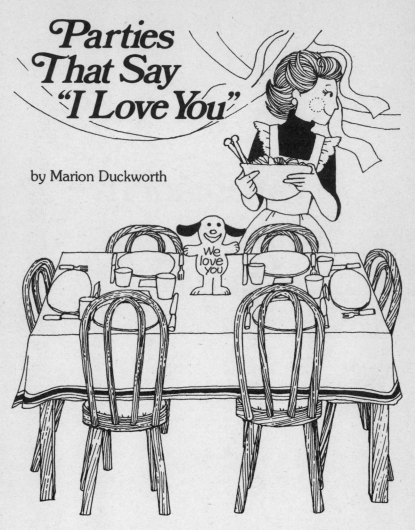

It was almost time. One of our sons was standing on a chair hanging orange crepe-paper streamers from the living room ceiling. A second son was blowing up balloons and tying them in clusters. The table had been set for dinner. Place cards, hand-lettered and decorated with pic-

tures of Snoopy cut from the comic strips, were set by each plate.

A third son, the guest of honor, was coming up the back steps. We ran to meet him and burst out in unison: "Surprise!"

A birthday? A welcome home party? No! We were giving him a "we love you" party.

Although we have the usual kinds of celebrations, too, these family parties have become special ways for us to say "we appreciate you." Some are simply "we love you" celebrations; others are "unbirthday parties." It isn't *really* the guest of honor's birthday, but why not celebrate an unbirthday too?

These celebrations grew from an idea that my husband had several years ago when we felt a special need to show our love to one of our sons. "Let's give him a party," my husband suggested. "We'll just have the family."

"But what kind of party?" I wanted to know.

"We'll call it an unbirthday party," he decided. And the tradition began.

We are one of America's nuclear families living thousands of miles from aunts, uncles, grandparents and cousins—family members whose affections would provide security and strengthen our sons' self-images. These parties help provide the supportive emotional nourishment necessary for families in this situation. Every spontaneous display of love reinforces the individual's view of himself as significant. It also helps him see himself as God sees him—as a worthwhile individual. Given when they are needed, our parties have often proved to be an encouragement during a difficult time.

The "you-are-special" celebrations are never elaborate and call upon every family member's ingenuity to make them successful. Little money is spent. The idea is to be as creative as possible. Working separately, each of us makes signs and banners, using crayons, felt pens and pictures cut from magazines. Later we come together to share what we've made. As we work, we ask ourselves: What is special about that person? What nice thing would I like to say? We make our pictures, signs and slogans as original as we can. Signs have read: "Accept no substitutes. John is the original nice guy," and "Mark is Number One; vote for him." And at every party, there are some signs that say simply: "We love you."

We decide on the menu, choosing dinners that are the honored person's favorite. In our house that usually means spaghetti and meatballs. Desserts run from ice cream to banana cream pie.

If there are gifts, they are tiny, inexpensive items wrapped in tissue and hidden in a cardboard carton filled with wadded-up newspapers. We call this "a surprise box." The celebrator must sort through the newspapers to find his gifts: a package of cupcakes, perhaps a magazine, a box of crayons and a ball.

Entertainment is spontaneous. Conversation centers around the honored guest and his special interests. Sometimes we reminisce about "when you were little." The boys may play their guitars and sing. We may play games. Whatever we do—talk, sing, eat, give gifts, decorate—we try to tell our honored guest that "you are part of us. We think you are very special."

I remember a day that called for a "you-are-special" celebration. The day began at four in the morning when one of our sons dragged himself out of bed to catch a bus that would take him to the field to work as temporary farm labor that first morning of the strawberry-picking season. From our own experiences, the rest of us could remember how he felt: sleepy, shivering in the early morning chill, aching as he kneeled for hours over rows of strawberries; and later in the day sweating under a blazing sun. It was time for a party!

That afternoon we got ready. By the time we watched him slowly climb the back steps, his clothes red with strawberry stain and black with mud, the table was set, the food was nearly done, signs and decorations were hung, and a box of tiny gifts was hidden in a carton between wads of newspapers. He opened the back door and stood still for a moment, his face streaked with sweat and dirt, and his sweat shirt tied around his waist. Then, when we all jumped out in front of him and yelled "Surprise!" a broad grin crept across his face. One of us ran his bath, another found clean clothes, still another brushed the mud from his tennis shoes.

Then he walked through the house reading the signs we'd made and stopped in front of the kitchen stove to inspect the contents of the simmering pots. The party reminded him that, while out on the farm he might be just one of the hands, here at home he was important and we appreciated him and his perseverance. And as we busied ourselves making him comfortable, we were drawn to one another in the bonds of family love.

My husband and I have both been the guest of honor at family celebrations, too. On one occasion, when my husband had been working harder than usual, one of our sons suggested a party for him. Our signs expressed how we felt. One read: "Mr. Duckworth, we have just one word to say to you: THANKS." Another sign was illustrated with a cartoon character and said: "Whenever I'm in a bad mood, just seeing Mr. Duckworth makes me feel good. He's the greatest guy in the entire world."

On another occasion, we were vacationing in a borrowed cabin on the shore when my husband received word that he had to return to work for the day. He left very early in the morning to begin the long drive. This was his only vacation all year and his professional responsibilities had taken a slice out of the middle of it.

Time for a party! In the cabin we really had to improvise.

What materials did we have to use? Scrap paper, crayons and ball-point pens. Far from a store and without transportation, I examined the cupboards and refrigerator and began to plan the menu. As we worked, we talked about our father and husband and what he meant to us.

He returned home that evening to signs printed with crayon on notebook paper that read: "We love you." As we sat in front of the window that overlooked the beach, eating our "special" dinner, he looked at each one of us and said, "You make it all worthwhile."

At some time, each one of us has needed to be reminded that we are important to the rest of our family just because of who we are: not because we have earned straight A's in school, have been recognized by our peers as an outstanding athlete, or have been made president of our class, club or company. Parties that have communicated "we appreciate you," given when we most needed them, are the ones that have touched us most deeply. In our house, "let's have a party" usually means "let's let someone know how much we love him." And our love for one another is, after all, something to celebrate.

Our Birthday Traditions

by Phyllis Stanley

Building traditions is one of our ways of providing myriads of happy memories in the hearts of our children. First as a military family and now as missionaries, we have made many moves and our children have spent a good part of their lives in foreign lands.

Although our children will not have geographical roots, we pray that the richness of tradition in our home will give them a deep sense of belonging, no matter where we may live. We feel birthdays are a time of happy celebrating. It's a joyful time of telling our children that God has given us the fun of being their parents.

Every year our most important gift to our birthday child is prayer, because it is an investment into his life for eternity. On the birthday morning, my husband and I arise an hour earlier to pray specifically for the child. We pray for his future, his mate, his education, his friends, his growth in Christ and his character. We also read together passages of Scripture. That hour passes so quickly, and the day begins with a bubble of joy in our hearts.

Because of our Scandinavian background, our favorite tradition is serving breakfast in bed. I always make a special coffee cake in the shape of the child's age, arrange it on a lovely tray amidst mugs of hot chocolate and tea and a tall candle that brightens the darkness of the winter morning birthdays. Then, as a family we tiptoe to the bedroom door, breaking out in unison, "Happy birthday to you!" As the children share their homemade cards and sweet original poems, Daddy flashes his camera and there's a bit of magic in the air.

All of the birthday cards, many from thousands of miles away, are carefully read aloud to be enjoyed by everyone. Then, I always read the story of their birthday. Each child's

story tells how he had been asked for from the Lord, the tears of joy and gratefulness Daddy and I experienced in hearing their first cry, the warmth of holding them in our arms and the happiness we felt because they were born into our family. The stories never grow old, and all the children are always eager to hear the "birthday" stories.

When the children are old enough, we let them plan an afternoon party for their friends. We've had doll parties, peanut parties, pizza parties, slumber parties, swimming parties and scavenger hunts. Sometimes the planning is almost as much fun as the party!

In the evening, we have a simple "family party." The birthday child chooses his own menu. Each member of the family brings a small gift wrapped in foil. The child's age is incorporated into the gift. For example, if the child is 10 years old, one gift may be 10 pennies, or 10 pieces of gum or 10 raisins in a matchbox. These gifts help the child to appreciate the joy of receiving even little gifts that are given with love.

One of our favorite family birthday games is the Balloon Game. Before our family party we put notes in each balloon. Each person must sit on a balloon to break it and then follow the instructions on the note. The kids think it's hilarious to see Dad doing a somersault, blowing the biggest bubble possible with bubble gum, or mooing like a cow. After all the festivities, we all take turns thanking God for the birthday child.

Our birthday preparations take a lot of time, but we love making this happy, memory-making investment in each child's life and we pray it will produce in their lives fruits of love, appreciation and the joy of giving.

For now, our reward is the happy smile as our birthday child says, "I'm so glad I'm in our family. This is the happiest birthday I've ever had!"

Happy Birthday, Mom!

by Penny V. Schwab

Everything went wrong on my birthday.

I woke up sneezing. Spring flowers are beautiful, but aggravating to hay fever victims!

Instead of cheery cards, the morning mail brought bills and more bills.

I spent the afternoon hauling tanks of nitrogen fertilizer for my farmer-husband.

While I was gone, the dogs cornered and killed Tiger, my favorite cat.

As I prepared supper that evening, my outlook on life was bleak. At 30 I was no longer a part of the "now" generation. What happened to my youth? What had I accomplished? What could I look forward to if I lived another 30 years?

Even my spiritual life seemed dismal and unproductive. God had called several of my friends to exciting ministries. A college classmate was a medical missionary in the Gaza Strip. A couple from our community were serving at a children's hospital in Haiti. Other friends were leading large groups in worship and prayer.

And me. I was doing the same old things I'd always done—attending a Bible study and prayer group, playing the organ for church worship services, teaching Bible school, baking pies for church suppers. All things that were necessary, perhaps, but so insignificant!

The children didn't notice my gloomy mood. There was much grinning and giggling as they sat down to eat.

"HAPPY BIRTHDAY, MOM!" they all shouted at once. The boys pulled clumsily wrapped packages from behind their backs and proudly handed them to me.

Patrick's gift was stationery. "I thought plain white would be best," he said with typical nine-year-old practicality. "The paper shaped like overalls wouldn't fit in your typewriter."

Michael, age seven, had chosen a pair of red spiral candles. "I wanted to buy an orange and black cat statue left over from Halloween," he said seriously, "but even marked down twice it was still three dollars. I just had 75 cents."

"I'm glad you got the candles," I told him. Even though it wasn't completely dark, we lighted them. Their warm glow gave the meal some semblance of cheer.

Rebecca, our five-year-old daughter, didn't have a gift. "I wanted to give you the best present," she said sadly. "Something bigger and importanter than stationery or candles. But I couldn't find anything."

I held her close, assuring her I understood and that I hadn't expected a present anyway. After the children left the table, though, I spent awhile thinking about what Rebecca had said.

Was I acting like a five-year-old with regard to my family, to Christian service, to life? Was I so anxious for my contributions to be "bigger and importanter" than other people's that I neglected my designated tasks?

The parable of the three stewards flashed into my mind. I'd read it many times. Yet as I took my Bible and studied the twenty-fifth chapter of Matthew, the words took on a whole new meaning. Especially verse 29: "For the man who uses well what he is given shall be given more, and he shall have abundance. But from the man who is unfaithful, even what little... he has shall be taken from him" *(The Living Bible)*.

I hadn't buried my talents as the unfaithful steward had done. But too often I had failed to do my best with the talents and tasks I'd been given.

Instead of thanking God for the physical strength to work alongside my husband, I resented the extra jobs. Instead of praising the Lord for the extra measures of closeness that comes from shared lifework (and remembering the countless times my husband helped me!), I grumbled about interruptions in my household schedule.

Our children held perfect attendance pins from Sunday School, but I realized I was neglecting their spiritual training at home. Too frequently family Bible study and prayer had been replaced by, "You boys read Rebecca a Bible story! And say your prayers!" Just as important, I was overlooking opportunities to talk with the children about themselves, about God, and about the world around them.

My musical talents are modest. Was I cheerfully using the ability I did have, though? Well, not exactly cheerfully. My answer to, "Will you play the organ again on Sunday?" was sometimes a grudging, "Yes, if you can't possibly find anyone else." I always helped with Bible school, but I sometimes thought more about the people who wouldn't help than about teaching children to love and serve the Lord.

I looked again at my birthday gifts from the children—a box of plain white stationery and two red candles. In their small gestures of love, my children had given a far more valuable gift than they realized—the realization that God did not require great and wonderful things from me. He, in His infinite wisdom, has given me my talents and my tasks. He asks only that I be faithful to the responsibilities that are mine.

I got up with a renewed sense of commitment. Maybe God would call me to new, exciting areas of service. If so, I prayed I'd be ready to meet the challenge. But if the next 30 years held a continuation of small tasks, of lowly service, I'd welcome that too. I'd find joy, fulfillment, even adventure in those little things which done in His name make up a complete, worthwhile life.

—From *Alive* magazine, July/August, 1974. Mennonite Broadcasts, Inc. Reprinted by permission.

Time to Plan
for Family Fun

Many parents—already loaded with other duties and problems—are hardly aware that family recreation is part of their responsibility. Also, it is one of their best tools for creating the family togetherness they need.

Top-level family fun requires planning. It is true that some outstanding good times are unplanned and take place by a sort of spontaneous combustion. But the best family recreation is the result of at least some degree of advance thought.

Family fun requires not only time, effort and planning, but also a philosophical acceptance of some degree of household disorder and mess. If your home has to be so spic and span that your children don't feel free to have a good time in it... then you will probably soon find your children looking for their good times somewhere else.

—From *How to Keep Your Family Together and Still Have Fun,* Marion Leach Jacobsen (Zondervan, 1971). Used by permission.

Family Fun Planner

Use a Family Fun Planner (see Fig. 1) and have some family fun planning family activities for the next four weeks.

See Week 1 (top section) for an example of how the Family Fun Planner works. The blocks on the left side represent days of the week. The lines on the right side are

Family Fun Planner **

Fig.1

1 week

S	M	T	W	T	F	S	
							Read together
							Company
		X			X		Bike ride
				X			Ice-cream cone
			X				Family night
							Window shop
							Take a mystery trip

2 week

S	M	T	W	T	F	S	

3 week

S	M	T	W	T	F	S	

4 week

S	M	T	W	T	F	S	

**All items marked with ** are from family time ideas developed by Wayne Rickerson, author of *Good Times for Your Family* (Regal Books, 1976). Used by permission.

for listing possible family activities. The family puts a check mark in the block under the preferred day on the same line with the selected activity. For example, Week 1 shows Family Time as the selected activity for Wednesday.

Ask family members to suggest possible activities for the other weeks. (You may want to repeat some of the activities on a weekly basis.) Write the activities in Weeks 2,3 and 4 and then decide as a family when you will do at least one activity for each week. Post your Family Fun Planner in a central location. Take time each month to plan for family activities.**

Family Fun Coupons

Discover how your ideas of family fun and your children's ideas can be worked into your family's schedule by having a family fun coupon exchange (see Fig. 2). Give children time to make six coupons for activities they think would be fun to do with or for the family. At the same time Mother and Dad make six coupons for activities they think would be fun to do with their children.

When coupons are complete, take turns drawing from each pile and deciding how and when to include the different activities into the family schedule.

Even very young children will enjoy the Family Fun Coupons. Make certain some of the activities on the coupons are things the younger child will enjoy.**

Just for Fun

Use the following ideas for times of recreation and fun on your family nights—after your meal and Bible sharing activities:

- Work a jigsaw puzzle.
- Have a "family program": with everyone—from littlest to oldest—sharing something he likes to do. (In one

FAMILY FUN TIME COUPON

This coupon entitles you to treat the family to an ice-cream cone. (Dad will pay, of course.)

" ...be like one big happy family...loving one another with tender hearts. "

I Peter 3:8

FAMILY FUN TIME COUPON

This coupon entitles you to choose a special family dinner and help cook it.

"A brother(sister) is born to help."

Proverbs 17:17

** Fig. 2

family such a program included a head stand, a flute solo, two jokes and an original poem.)

● Get together ingredients for a simple (and good to eat) cookie recipe and have a family cookie bake. Warm cookies and cold milk make a treat for any family.

• Use numbers for a bit of fun. Have everyone write down his house number. Double it. Add 5. Multiply by 50. Add his age. Add 365, and subtract 615. Magic! The house number is on the left and the correct age on the right. (For young ones, you do the math.)

• Prepare a box of small construction paper shapes: squares, triangles, rectangles, circles, ovals, etc. Give each person in the family a blank piece of paper, glue or paste and let each one create his own original design.

• Measure everyone in the family for height. Record feet and inches and put the record away for a year. Delegate someone in the family to call for a recheck a year from this date. Then you can discover how much growing happened in a year! How much do people grow in a year?

• Get out photos of when Mom and Dad were in school. Have styles changed? Dresses, suits, hair?

• Leave the TV off, unless (and only unless) there is a truly good program to watch and enjoy together.

• Play Ping-Pong Bounce. Fasten three or four empty coffee cans together with string or rubber bands. Label each coffee can with a different score value: 5, 10, 15, 25. Take turns bouncing three balls into the cans with a scorekeeper jotting down the score each person makes. After everyone has had four turns, total the score.

• Play Rattle and Guess. Before family night, get together a number of boxes with lids. (Oatmeal boxes are just right.) In each box place an object (or objects that are alike), for example, keys, coins, beans, rice, macaroni, etc. Tape on lid and number each box. Divide family into pairs (younger with older) to work with boxes shaking, deciding and listing what is in each one. After decisions are made, have Dad open boxes and reveal what is really inside each one.

• Stone Stuff. Gather around a table with supplies for

making your own stone stuff originals. You will need rocks and pebbles of different sizes, white glue, felt scraps, yarn pieces, bits of cloth, etc. The point is: don't paint your stone, trim it. Glue the trimmed stone to a scrapwood background and you'll have an interesting plaque.

• Penny Hunt. Hide pennies throughout a specified area such as the yard, patio, family room, downstairs, or such. Remind everyone that all pennies are hidden *in sight* (if you look carefully). There are none in drawers, cupboards, etc. Also, pennies wrapped in foil can be exchanged for dimes. At the word GO everyone starts the hunt and continues until the STOP whistle; then everyone comes together for the penny count. Tip: give each person a plastic bag for collecting pennies during the hunt.

• Peanut Race. Divide family into two teams. Players must carry an unshelled peanut between their knees. The team with everyone crossing the finish line first, wins.

• Bible Story Drawings and Doodles. After you read a Bible story with your family give everyone time to create a drawing or doodle that expresses something about the story.

Doodles are a fun way to express feelings. Let your family know that artistic talent is not required, only the willingness to make a design or doodle that some way shows how a person feels.

The real value of doodles comes as family members explain their doodles to the rest of the family group, describing how they express the feelings in the Bible story.

Possible stories to doodle or draw include: Joseph and His Brothers; Daniel in the Lion's Den; Jonah and the Big Fish; David and Goliath; The Good Samaritan; The Blind Man Made to See. In fact, almost any Bible story involving emotions and feelings that your child can understand can be used.

Fun and Games for the Flu Season

by Rhonda Casey

It's difficult to be a patient, loving parent during the flu season. After three or four days of interrupted sleep, taking temperatures, coaxing down medicines and making chicken soup, the Christian mother may feel Paul's love chapter certainly wasn't meant for mothers of sick children. Indeed, the day the sick and afflicted return to school, she may take to her bed, muttering she'd rather die than cook another pot of chicken soup.

But getting through the flu season (or a case of chicken pox!) needn't be such a trial this year—and it *could* even have its pleasant moments. Simply try a few of these easy-to-do games and crafts. You'll find sick days are easier for both mother and child when there are interesting things to do and amusing games to play.

Bedside box

Prepare a box of items that the sick child can use for handcrafts, so when he starts a project, everything is handy. Find a large box, about four or five inches deep. Let your child cover it with adhesive paper, decorate it with crayons or cut-out magazine pictures. Into the box place small scissors, crayons, cellophane tape, string, glue, brass fasteners, bits of fabric, yarn, buttons, old jewelry, etc.

Lapboard

Some kind of lapboard is needed for sickbed projects. You can use the top of a TV tray, a table leaf resting on two chairs (one on either side of the bed), a cardboard box with the sides shaped to fit over the child's lap (see Fig. 3), or even a cookie sheet. With the bedside box and lapboard, your child is ready for hours of bedtime fun.

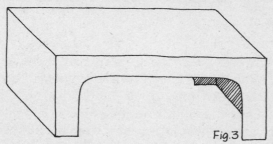

Fig. 3

Medicine-Time Clock

Children enjoy making a clock that can be set for their next dose of medicine. (This helps forgetful mothers too!) The child draws clock numbers on a paper plate and decorates the face using colored paper, decorative stickers, fabric, lace, etc. The clock hands are made from colored paper and are attached to the clock with brass paper fasteners. Presto! A beautiful reminder for your child to take his medicine.

Bedside Hide-and-Seek

This is a quick little game that can brighten up a dull afternoon. Mother says, "I'm hiding somewhere in this room. Guess where I'm hiding." As the child guesses, Mother gives the clue, "You're getting warmer" or "You're getting colder." After he "finds you," it's his turn to "hide."

Scrapbook

Children love to cut and paste. So this project will delight most shut-ins. The scrapbook can be very simple for preschoolers—cutting pictures out of magazines and pasting them in the scrapbook—or more sophisticated for the older child, who may prefer to write stories, poems, or keep a diary.

Use two pieces of cardboard for covers. (These can be from soap or cereal boxes.) The child pastes paper over the cardboard and then decorates them. Inside place several pieces of white and colored paper, make two holes in the left edge, and bind with pretty string or yarn.

Library Surprise Books

This is not a craft, but it is an activity the sick child will welcome. When Father is home with the children, take a quick trip to the library. Load up with an assortment of picture books for your child—his own collection of surprise books. Give him one or two each day while he is ill. (If you read them to him, he will be even more interested.) He may want to draw a picture about his favorite character, or even "write" his own book in pictures.

Bookmarks

If you have used the Library Surprise idea, your child may want to make bookmarks and decorate them in his own special way. Cut strips of colored paper about 2x6-inches. Then your child can "dress these up," using materials from his bedside box.

Collages from This and That

Now is the time to gather up old jewelry, buttons, macaroni, fabric scraps, and other items that would make a pretty collage. The child pastes items on colored cardboard or cardboard with colored paper pasted on. (Cardboard is recommended because it gives a stiff backing for the collage.) Buttons, jewelry, cloth, etc., combine to give a lovely effect. Collages are especially satisfying to preschoolers, who often are frustrated at their inability to draw like older brother or sister. In this project, the more abstract the better! (See Fig. 4.)

Fig. 4

Photo Albums

This is an activity that never fails to entertain children. No matter how many times they have looked through the family photo albums, youngsters are always fascinated at the way Mom and Dad used to look, and to find that Grandma and Grandpa were little once, too.

Hammer, Nails, Wood Scraps

If your child is almost well, but still has to take it easy, he may enjoy sitting on the floor hammering nails into boards you have provided, or even making a simple structure out of scrap lumber. (Most lumberyards are more than happy to get rid of scraps.) If it's warm enough in the garage, this is a perfect place to build. If not, the project can be done in the family living area if proper care is taken. This is great therapy for a child who has been forced, because of illness, to be still for several days. He can hammer away a little of that pent-up energy!

Next time someone comes down with a bug, see how many good hours you and your sick one can enjoy while you are at home together.

Family Prayer
Is a Celebration

by Mary C. Hopkins

It was a biting cold Montana day, with heavily drifted snow. However, the frigidness of the outdoors could not begin to affect the warmth and joy in the hearts of the McCormick family, for today Grandma and Grandpa would be arriving for a long-awaited visit.

Everyone in the McCormick household was attempting in one way or another to make this a very special day. Patrick and Mary Ellen had seen to it that each of their five children had a specific responsibility to carry out while they stepped out for a brief time to do some last-minute shopping.

However, upon returning, Pat and Mary Ellen found that the children had not finished their tasks and an air of coldness and bitterness had begun to set in. The scalloped potatoes, which the oldest daughter, Sue, was supposed to be watching, had boiled over and burned. John, the next oldest, had neglected to watch over baby Paul who was screaming, because two-year-old Marie was giving her younger brother some "loving" attention. Therefore, John was screaming at both Marie and Paul, neither of whom understood his outrage. Last but not least, Anne, the first-grader, couldn't find her favorite doll, and since no one else would listen to her, she ended up taking her frustration out on the dog. She was kicking the dog when her parents arrived home.

37

Mary Ellen was terribly disappointed that the dish of potatoes she had so carefully prepared was ruined, and had some rather harsh words for Sue. Upon surveying the complete situation, however, she soon realized that the potatoes could always be replaced, but what about the coldness and bitterness in the hearts, and what kind of atmosphere was this to bring Grandpa and Grandma into?

There was only one answer—to attempt to recreate the warmth, joy and peace that had existed earlier. Mary Ellen summoned all into the living room, asking them to join into a circle while placing baby Paul on the couch nearby.

The family knew why they had been called together, so Mary Ellen, referring to a reconciliation celebration, began, "God, we are here now to tell you and each person here that we have not loved enough, that we have heard your Word and have not lived its message as fully as we might have. We call out to you for renewed strength to continue to live and to love."

Pat then read a selection from Scripture, Matthew 6:14: "If you forgive others their failings, your heavenly Father will forgive you yours; but if you do not forgive others, your Father will not forgive your failings either" *(The Jerusalem Bible).*

Those in the family circle then joined hands and Mary Ellen asked forgiveness for her harsh words to Sue, and

Sue in turn asked to be forgiven for not tending to the potatoes. Pat said he was sorry for being impatient with Mary Ellen while shopping for groceries, followed by John who apologized for screaming at Marie and Paul. Anne's eyes wandered outside the circle where the dog was licking his wound and said, "I kicked Blackie and hurt him. I'm sorry."

Happy, unintelligible sounds could be heard from baby Paul as he was being kissed by Marie who had wandered from the circle. With that the McCormick family broke into song "Make me a channel of your peace...." Warmth, joy and peace once again filled the McCormick house and Grandpa and Grandma were welcomed with joy.

The McCormick family celebration, which actually took place, brings to life the true meaning of family prayer. It may not be the type of family prayer that you and I experienced in our growing-up years, but it speaks of the fact that family prayer and celebration are as important today as they were in times past. Many families are looking for new methods of praying together, and because of their desire and creativity they are adding a new dimension to family prayer... as family members gather together to talk with God.

—From *New Catholic World*. Copyright 1972 by the Missionary Society of St. Paul the Apostle in the State of New York. Used by permission.

Families Go Better with Prayer

by Gwen Fodge

Here's a variety of ways prayer can become a natural and joyful part of family life at your house. As you read the ideas check the ones you want to try with your family.

• Memorize a Bible verse that says something about prayer. Read the following verses together and as a family choose which you want to learn: Jeremiah 33:3; Psalm 91:15; Philippians 4:6.

• Occasionally, before the mealtime prayer of thanks, encourage each person to name something he/she is thankful for. These "notes of praise" will range from Susie's new puppy, to food on the table, to Dad's raise. God wants us to thank Him for everything! The first time you add this thanksgiving time to your mealtime prayer, read 1 Thessalonians 5:18 together.

• Is your toddler afraid to be left alone in his bedroom at night? Instead of being impatient with him, why not take time to talk to him about how Jesus loves him and cares for him? Say, with your child, the Bible words, "God cares about you" (see 1 Pet. 5:7). Pray with your youngster and encourage him to tell Jesus that he is afraid and wants Jesus to take care of him.

• Spend a little personal time with your children before they go to bed and always pray with each child at bedtime. Encourage your children to talk with God, telling Him about their day, thanking Him, and asking for personal help.

• Before family time prayers, some evening, form a family circle. Ask each person to give a thoughtful prayer request for the one sitting on his left. For example: Johnny says, "We could pray that God will help Sue remember all she has studied for that algebra test tomorrow." Sue says, "Let's pray that Dad will have a safe trip to and from work every day." Dad says, "I want to ask God to help Mom feel better today—she just can't do all she wants to get done with that headache." And Mom says, "I'm going to pray that Johnny's team has a good game; with everyone on the team playing their best." If you feel it is difficult or uncomfortable for your family to pray aloud for each other, have a time of silent prayer followed by Dad or Mom praying for everyone in the family. Also, what about promising each other to pray for one another during the coming day? Days go better when a person knows his family is praying about the rough spots!

Choose Your Prayer for Today

Prepare copies of the "prayer words" form below for members of your family. Take time to explain the columns of words as: how you feel about God; how you feel about yourself and what you want to say to God. Encourage each person to choose a word from each column to create a prayer that expresses a true feeling. Give everyone time to write out his prayer at the bottom of the page. Share your prayers with each other. Example circled below reads: Loving Father your struggling follower asks for courage.

Title for God		Title for Myself		My Message	
Dear	God	your sinful	servant	needs	help
Heavenly	Father	your frightened	son	begs for	advice
Gentle	Son	your confident	daughter	thanks for	forgiveness
Kind	Spirit	your fearful	child	asks for	you
Forgiving	Creator	your sorrowful	creature	requests	courage
Loving	Jesus	your grateful	brother	appreciates	confidence
Just	Christ	your confused	sister	enjoys	faith
Mysterious	Saviour	your joyful	follower	pleads for	patience
Unseen	Redeemer	your eager	believer	has	peace
Merciful	Friend	your angry	Christian	deserves	an answer
Powerful	Protector	your peaceful	disciple	searches for	understanding
Faithful	Judge	your struggling	prodigal	hopes for	friendship
All wise	Master	your determined	friend	fears	strength
Patient	Brother	your lonely	seeker	loves	generosity
Trusting	Guide	your faithful	minister	longs for	love

—From *Simulation Games for Religious Education,* Richard Reichert, St. Mary's College Press, p. 69. Used by permission.

Celebrate Being a Family

Try one of the following activities to help your family work together with 1 Peter 3:8-12, a Scripture passage rich with practical ideas for building a happy family.

Getting to Know You Better

Make copies of 1 Peter 3:8-12 from *The Living Bible* paraphrase (see box) so each two people in your family have a copy to share. Read the Scripture portion together.

Family Happiness 1 Peter 3:8-12 from *The Living Bible*

8. And now this word to all of you: You should be like one big happy family, full of sympathy toward each other, loving one another with tender hearts and humble minds.

9. Don't repay evil for evil. Don't snap back at those who say unkind things about you. Instead, pray for God's help for them, for we are to be kind to others, and God will bless us for it.

10. If you want a happy, good life, keep control of your tongue, and guard your lips from telling lies.

11. Turn away from evil and do good. Try to live in peace even if you must run after it to catch and hold it!

12. For the Lord is watching his children, listening to their prayers; but the Lord's face is hard against those who do evil.

Get ideas on what different ones see in the verses that are helpful ideas for building a happy family. Then comment: "It helps people be a happy family when they know each other better. People need to know what others in the family like and what they don't like. We all need to know what is important to each other. That's why we're going to share important things about ourselves as we play 'Getting to Know You Better.'"

To play, you will need a box full of slips of paper on which you have typed or written the following unfinished statements: I want...I like...I don't like...I like to go to...My favorite hobby is...When I grow up I want to be...My favorite color is...My favorite food is...I am happiest when...I like to hear...(Make two copies of each.)

Go around the family circle twice, giving each person the opportunity to complete two statements about himself. (If people are still having fun, continue, but do stop while everyone is still feeling good about sharing.)

Conclude this part of family night by joining hands and singing a favorite song together. Also pray, thanking God for the different kinds of people in your family.

Sharing Love—Breaking Bread

Have a special family meal that is more than eating food. First, instead of having the usual mealtime prayer, read 1 Peter 3:8-12 by having each person in the family read the verse (or part of a verse) you have written out and put at his place. Then enjoy a favorite casserole or some other simple dish the entire family enjoys. Make it an enjoyable meal as you share interesting happenings (and avoid usual tension areas!). Then, before dessert have a "Breaking Bread-Sharing Love" time.

Take a small uncut loaf of bread (even a hamburger bun

or roll will do). Dad or Mother breaks off a small piece of bread and offers it to the other with a loving statement and blessing, such as, "I'm glad we're together in our family. I love you." After the other person eats his piece of bread he takes the loaf, breaks off another piece and gives it to the next person with his statement of love.

Mother and Dad should share first so the younger members of the family will understand. Do not object if children all say the same thing as long as they're expressing a loving thought.

After you have all shared the bread, talk about how it takes more than one person to make a happy family. God's Word says, "Love one another." People need people to share love. People need people to share happiness. Take five minutes to list loving, sharing, helping ideas you would like to see working in your family. (For ideas read 1 Peter 3:8-12.)

Drama-time Teams

Divide the family into two teams. Be sure to include older and younger family members in each group. Give each team a copy of 1 Peter 3:8-12 in *The Living Bible* paraphrase (see box). Each team will also need the following instructions: (a) Choose something mentioned in this Scripture portion that you think is very important when it comes to making a family happy. (b) Decide together how you can act out the Bible idea so the other team can guess your choice. Use pantomime—silent acting—roleplay or any action that gets the idea across. (c) Also think through two reasons for your choice that you can share with the other team.

After both teams give their "act" and successfully guess the other team's choice, celebrate being a family as you share a family treat.

A Happy Family Is...

A Happy Family Is...Loving One Another
John 13:35—Christ's way
John 15:12—His commandment
1 Thessalonians 3:12—With His help
1 John 3:18,19—Really love...

A Happy Family Is...Being Full of Sympathy
Romans 15:1—Care for others
Galatians 6:2—Share their burdens
Philippians 2:1-4—Be unselfish
Romans 12:10—Think of others

A Happy Family Is...Not Repaying Evil for Evil
Luke 6:35—Be merciful
Luke 17:3—Forgive
Ephesians 4:32—Be tenderhearted
Colossians 3:13—Be gentle
Matthew 5:39-46—Love even enemies

A Happy Family Is...Keeping Control of Your Tongue
Proverbs 15:1—Turn away anger
Proverbs 18:8—Untruths can hurt
Ephesians 4:25-31—Speak truth with kindness
James 4:11—Don't criticize
1 Peter 3:8-10—Guard what you say

A Happy Family Is...Living in Peace
Psalm 133:1—How good it is!
Proverbs 17:1—Peace makes life good
Matthew 5:9—Be a peacemaker
Romans 12:18—Be at peace yourself
1 Thessalonians 5:13—Peace for you...
1 Peter 3:8-12—Live in peace always

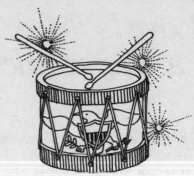

Celebrate—
Make It a
Special Day

Love Is More than a Paper Valentine

by Don Highlander

Early one February Saturday morning I hurried downstairs to my office hideout. I was frantically trying to catch up on about 12 hours of work in the following 8 hours. I had been traveling for two weeks. Where would I begin? I began to make a list of priorities: Write up reports. Answer the mail. Return phone calls. Plan for the coming week seminars. Finish some yard work and repairs. Buy valentines for the kids and my wife. Wait! I had wanted to write my own this year. It would take a little time but, perhaps, not as long as shopping for some.

I turned to 1 Corinthians 13, the love chapter in the Bible. Certainly there would be some inspiration there. Indeed, personal meditation would be a good way also to start a busy day. It would have to be accomplished quickly, but it would be helpful to seek God's love, joy and peace to guide my attitudes for the day. I had learned that if I had the right attitude and motivation that I could accomplish twice as much in a day's work.

I began to record my thoughts when I heard footsteps.

"Daddy, what are you doing up so early?"

I sharply returned the same question. "What are *you* doing up so early?"

My six-year-old daughter replied, "I want to sit on your lap and read the Bible with you. I missed you while you were gone."

Now how could I handle that one? I almost snapped back with a loud "No," and "It's back to bed for you."

But what about the caring concern about which I had just read: *If I have not love, I am nothing. . . . Love is very patient and kind. . . . Love is never selfish or rude. . . . Love is not irritable or touchy. . . . Let love be your greatest aim.*

Could I respond in a loving, consistent way? Was God's grace sufficient? I smiled and held out my arms.

My daughter climbed upon my lap and "together" we composed the following as a morning psalm of praise to our heavenly Father. Later I had "our valentine" printed on parchment in order to share our early morning experience with others.

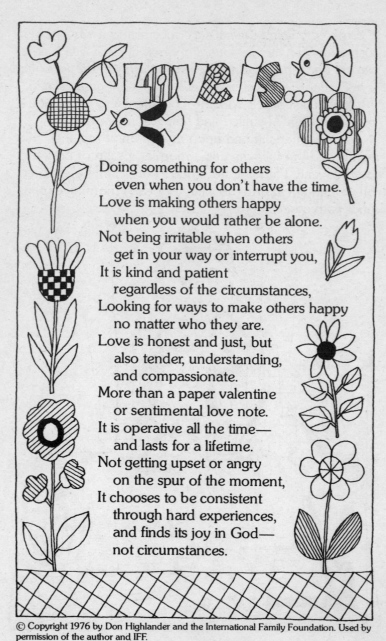

Love is...

Doing something for others
even when you don't have the time.
Love is making others happy
when you would rather be alone.
Not being irritable when others
get in your way or interrupt you,
It is kind and patient
regardless of the circumstances,
Looking for ways to make others happy
no matter who they are.
Love is honest and just, but
also tender, understanding,
and compassionate.
More than a paper valentine
or sentimental love note.
It is operative all the time—
and lasts for a lifetime.
Not getting upset or angry
on the spur of the moment,
It chooses to be consistent
through hard experiences,
and finds its joy in God—
not circumstances.

Decorate for Valentine's Day

Valentine decorations all through the house say in a happy way, "We're having a good time! We love each other. We're celebrating!"

If you supply your children with the "makings," they will come up with bright decorations plus valentines to give one another. Build on these ideas:

• Banners can be made from many kinds of material. Let your youngsters design their own banners using large sheets of paper, red yarn, paper doilies, fabric scraps and wallpaper samples (see Fig. 5).

Fig.5

• A sparkly valentine mobile is simple to make. Cut a cardboard outline of a large heart. Make smaller foil hearts with red construction paper rims to hang from the cardboard outline. Use red yarn for attaching the hearts and hanging the mobile (see Fig. 6).

• Simple but pretty valentines for decorations (or for giving) can be made by cutting hearts from red construction paper. Outline the paper hearts with glue. While the glue is still wet go around the edge of the heart with heavy white yarn. Allow enough yarn for tying a bow after the glue dries (see Fig. 7).

Be my Valentine!

Fig. 7

Fig. 6

Happy Mother's Day

A Mother's Day celebration should be planned by everyone except Mother. Have a secret family meeting. Ask children to suggest ways to make Mother feel loved and appreciated.

Praise Mother

Have someone read Proverbs 31:28,29. Ask each person to tell what he feels this verse means.

Give each family member a sheet of paper. Write at the top, "Mom Is Marvelous." Explain that on the rest of the paper everyone is to make a list of the things they appreciate about Mother. This list might include personal qualities or things she does for the family and others. The list should be signed when completed.**

Honor Mother

Read Exodus 20:12. Talk for a few minutes about the meaning of the word honor. (The dictionary definition: "recognition and esteem shown to another." Help children to put this definition in their own words.) Then discuss:

1. Why do you think God instructed children to honor their mothers?

2. How can we honor Mother with our actions?

3. How can we honor Mother with our words?**

Mother's Wishing Well

Plan for ways to show appreciation for Mother in actions as well as words. Give each family member a sheet of paper. Have them write the following open-ended sentence near the top of the paper. "I will show appreciation for Mother by_____and_____." Then each member, in turn, should allow Mother two wishes. One wish might be, "What do you wish I would do around the house?" Another could be, "What attitude do you wish I would change?"

When a family member has asked Mother for her wishes he should write her request on the paper and sign his name, then work hard to fulfill those wishes!**

Filmstrip Fun

Ask at a camera store for empty film cans (enough so each family member can have one).

Family members will enjoy using felt pens and a 1½-inch strip of typing paper to make "filmstrips" for mother (see Fig. 8). Use frame 1 for the title, frame 2 for the name of the author and illustrator, and the rest of the frames to

Mom, I Love You!

Written and illustrated by KAREN

I will

THE END

Fig. 8

picture or write specific things you will do to show your love for Mom. Roll the finished "filmstrip" and put it in a film can. Label the can with your filmstrip title.

Young children can dictate their ideas to an older family member—or they can draw a large picture instead of making a filmstrip.

Make a Mother's Day Card

Dad and older members of the family may want to announce to Mother that she has 30 minutes to relax, read, or whatever—but she must go out of the room. While Mother is gone, work together to make a big "We Love Mother" card. Fold an 11x17-inch piece of construction paper and letter on the front WE LOVE MOTHER...or some other message the family chooses. Inside, either paste a photo of each person or have each one draw his own picture to paste in the card. Leave room for each person to sign his name or to write a short love message (see Fig. 9). Now call Mother into the room and let the youngest member of the family give the card to her.

Fig. 9

History of Mother

Encourage your older children to interview their mother to get better acquainted with her life. Following are questions to include in the interview:

1. Where were you born?
2. How many brothers and sisters did you have?
3. Were you the oldest or the youngest child?
4. How many different schools did you go to? Where were they located?
5. What were favorite things you liked to do when you were a child?
6. Can you remember one special toy? One special friend?

7. Did your family have a nickname for you?

8. Did you ever have a pet? If so, what was its name?

9. Can you remember different things you wanted to do when you grew up?

10. What was the funniest thing that ever happened to you?

Of course the "interviewers" can add as many of their own questions as they wish. Then plan a special Mother's Hour during the week when the older children serve a treat and share their "History of Mother" with everyone in the family.**

A Litany of Thanks

Read Psalm 136:1-4. Explain that this kind of prayer is called a litany. In a litany the leader says a sentence and then the rest of the people say a refrain—a group of words that is repeated over and over again. Ask your children to listen for the refrain as you read Psalm 136:1-4 again.

Write a litany telling God "thank you" for Mother. Have family members suggest five or six sentences like: "I like to do things with Mom" or "Mom takes care of me when I'm sick." List these sentences. Then have family members decide on a refrain—a short sentence that tells God thank you for Mom; for example, "Thank you, God, for Mom."

Practice saying your litany. Each time the leader reads a sentence from your list, the rest of the family says the refrain. Your litany might begin something like this:

Leader: I like to do things with Mom.

Family: Thank you, God, for Mom.

Leader: Mom takes care of me when I'm sick.

Family: Thank you, God, for Mom.

Continue the litany with ideas from each member of the family.

Make Dad's Day Special

Plan your Father's Day celebration when Dad isn't around. Have a secret meeting—with Dad left out. Encourage every family member to come up with ideas to make Dad feel appreciated and loved.

This Is Your Life, Dad

Blindfold Father and sit him down in his favorite chair. Then announce, "This Is Your Life, Dad!" and remove the blindfold.

Let Mother go first and recall when Father got married, where, what happened, etc. She might also recall events from courtship days and the engagement. Be sure to include some humorous anecdotes. Work in a positive thought from Scripture, a verse that has meant a lot to Mother and Father in their marriage.

Next, have someone ready to read Psalm 127:1-5. Then call on each child for his or her part in the "This Is Your Life" program. Have the oldest tell Father when he had his first child, where it was born, interesting things that happened, etc. Mother can supply plenty of information here, too.

Let other children participate, all telling Father when they were born, their name, etc. For example:

"In 1965 your second child arrived—Christy Ann— who weighed 8 lb. 8 oz. You made the trip to Memorial Hospital in record time and calmly received the news while drinking a cup of coffee in the hospital coffee shop. You were glad when Mother and Christy Ann got home from the hospital, though, because all the TV dinners were just about gone."

If possible, arrange for some special friends of Father to make a surprise appearance during the "This Is Your Life" program. Include them in the rest of the evening's activities.

After "This Is Your Life, Dad," bring out a special set of gifts for the guest of honor. The gifts are in the form of coupons (see Fig. 10) which each person, including Mother, gives to Father as a promise or guarantee to do a chore, a special favor, etc.

Mother and children lead in a prayer of thanksgiving for Father—his love, his care and for all he does for the family.

Fig. 10

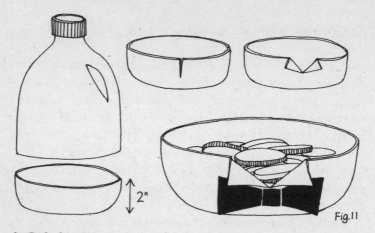

Fig.11

A Gift for Dad

Young children will enjoy making a simple change holder for Dad's dresser.

You'll need a plastic bottle with bottom measurement of about 4 inches, small pieces of felt for tie, stapler and scissors. Cut off plastic bottle so 2 inches remain. Cut slit 1 inch deep as shown. Fold at slit to make "shirt collar." Cut felt bow-tie shape. Staple in place under slit (see Fig. 11). Now all that's left to do is to give the gift to Father!

Who Knows Dad?

This activity will help stimulate more thinking about Dad. Give each person a pencil and paper. Have them number 1-10. Explain that you are going to ask 10 questions about Dad. One point will be given for each correct answer. Each person is to write his answer on the paper.

When the quiz is over, read the questions and have each family member give his answer. Then ask Dad for the correct answer. Have each person add up his own score. Who knew the most about Dad? *Quiz Questions:* What is Dad's favorite: fruit, hobby, hymn, Scripture verse, time of day, color, vegetable, sport, TV program, animal?**

Dad's Name Is the Game

Make an acrostic out of Dad's first name. Have each person write the letters of Dad's name vertically on a sheet of paper. Beside each letter write a word, starting with that letter. The word should describe him as shown in the example below.

> J Jolly
> O Open
> H Honest
> N Neat

Have each person read their acrostic to Dad.**

My Dad

Help your young child make a book titled *My Dad*. Either use a small notebook or staple several pieces of paper together. Give your child some magazines, scissors and glue. Have him look for pictures of fathers doing things his daddy does such as driving the car, mowing the lawn, eating with the family, playing with the children, talking with Mother, reading, etc. Help your youngster cut out the pictures and paste them in his book. Talk about the pictures and how important Dad is to the family.

Make the book a special present your child can give to his dad—and try to plan for time he/she can explain and talk about the pictures with Dad.**

Hand-some Man

Let one of the children trace the outline of Dad's hands on a large piece of poster board. Then have each member of the family draw a picture or write a note that shows appreciation for things that Dad does—gives hugs, fixes toys, plays games, fixes the car, reads stories, goes to work (whatever is suitable for your family). Finish the poster by

Fig. 12

lettering "Thank You, Dad" in large letters (see Fig. 12). Give the poster to Dad as a special father's day card.

Father's Day Projects

Your older children can choose from these special projects for remembering Dad on his special day.

1. *Create a slide show for Dad.*

If you have old exposed slides that no one cares about, you can remove the photograph on the slide with a cotton swab dipped in household bleach. The area will turn blue at first, but will become clear with more rubbing... and then you can put your picture on the slide. Draw on the slides with colored marking pens or acrylic paints.

You may even want to record a cassette to play while you show Dad the slides.

2. *Write a letter to Dad.* Make the letter a special thank you for good memories you've made together.

3. *Invite Dad out for a treat.* How about the older children pooling their ideas and resources and inviting Dad out for something he enjoys doing—bowling, a hike, a concert, a baseball game.

A Father's Day Card

A "necktie" card is fun for a young child to make and fun to give. Trace a tie outline on a piece of colored construction paper (see Fig. 13). Letter on the paper necktie: *I'm glad God gave me you for my Daddy.* Help your child paste a photo of himself near words.

Then, let your youngster cut out the necktie. Don't help unless your child asks for help. Those ragged edges are proof to Daddy that little hands made his card!

Fig. 13

School's Out— Celebrate the School Year

Plan a family celebration that centers around the past school year. Set aside some time as a family to "take stock" on the accomplishments of the past school year and to thank the Lord for the knowledge and wisdom He provides.

Talk about highlights of the school year: best accomplishments, most enjoyable subjects, the outstanding events, etc. Keep the conversation positive. Don't make it a big "put down" on school.

At the same time, don't make a big thing out of A's and awards at the expense of children who didn't get many (or any). For example, lavish praise of a child who has done well in school is bound to cut down the self-esteem of another who has had an average year. Your children have to do enough wrestling with the "grades game" during the year. For your celebration, let them relax and just enjoy the feeling of finishing another year of school, looking forward to summer, and enjoying themselves.

Talk together about school and what it means. What do we gain from school? (knowledge, wisdom, common sense). What has God given us so we can learn? (our minds, books, teachers). What is more important? Making a lot of money or living wisely? Refer everyone to Proverbs 3:13-21 in *The Living Bible:*

The man who knows right from wrong and has good judgment and common sense is happier than the man who is immensely rich! For such wisdom is far more valuable than precious jewels. Nothing else compares with it. Wisdom gives: a long, good life, riches, honor, pleasure, peace.

Wisdom is a tree of life to those who eat her fruit; happy is the man who keeps on eating it.

The Lord's wisdom founded the earth; his understanding established all the universe and space. The deep fountains of the earth were broken open by his knowledge, and the skies poured down rain.

Have two goals: wisdom—that is, knowing and doing right—and common sense. Don't let them slip away.

Talk about what the passage from Proverbs says. Why is wisdom more valuable than precious jewels? What two important goals are we trying to reach? (v. 21—knowing and doing right, and common sense).

How did the Lord make the earth—the universe? (by His wisdom, v. 19).

Thank God together for what He has done through His wisdom. Ask Him for wisdom to know and do the right thing, to use common sense.

Thank You Cards

One right (and nice) thing that the family could do at this time of year would be to send "thank you" cards to the teachers each child had in school this past year. Attractive "thank you" cards can be purchased, but it will be more fun and more meaningful if you make your own cards from simple materials. Use colored construction paper or good quality, plain white paper, plus felt-tip pens, to make a card like the one in Figure 14. Make a separate card for each teacher. Mother and Dad may want to sign the cards, too.

After signing the cards and sealing them in envelopes ready to mail, have another brief time of prayer for the teachers who will receive them. Give thanks for their work and dedication; pray for their physical and spiritual welfare.

Celebrate with an Ice Cream Cone

After you've addressed the cards (send them to the school if you don't have home addresses) take a family walk or ride and mail them. If you pass an ice-cream store celebrate "school-is-out" with an ice-cream cone for everyone.

This was a very GOOD year...

and you were a very GOOD teacher! Thank you, Jack

Fig. 14

It's the Fourth of July

The idea of celebrating Independence Day—July 4—with the family may leave some parents feeling ambivalent. Government and government officials have come under heavy criticism in recent years, and not without cause. The point that you can make, however, is that God has ordained (established) governments and that the Christian family's duty is to support them, even though they may make mistakes. In addition, there are still plenty of good things to be said about your country and much for which to be thankful.*

Celebrate with a Picnic

Get the family together and discuss several favorite picnic spots for your Fourth of July celebration (park, lake, hilly spot out in the country). When the selections are reduced to one per family member, letter names of places on slips of paper. Youngest member draws a slip to determine picnic location.

Use a patriotic motif for the picnic meal. The children could even try decorating a sheet cake as an American flag. Hotdogs, hamburgers, potato chips and other "All American" dishes can head the menu.

Pledge Allegiance to the Flag

During your Fourth of July celebration gather around

---

*Families living outside the U.S. can adapt these ideas to their own situations and needs.

the flag and pledge allegiance to the Stars and Stripes. Take time for the family to talk about what the pledge of allegiance means. When we say the Pledge of Allegiance what are we saying about ourselves and America? Discuss individual words: pledge; allegiance; liberty; justice. During the Fourth of July week have older children use the dictionary to find definitions of these key words.

Celebrate with a Parade

Young children will enjoy planning and participating in a neighborhood July 4th parade. Get together with parents of other youngsters in your neighborhood and see if the idea seems good to everyone. It won't take elaborate planning to come up with a parade that will delight the children. You will need red, white and blue paper hats, small American flags to wave, an older child or father to play a lively march on the trumpet and rhythm instruments for some enthusiastic noise. (Cake pans and spoons, covered coffee cans containing a handful of dried beans, etc.)

And at the end of the parade you will need plenty of cold lemonade!

Flag and Country

On a large sheet of paper draw a replica of the American flag. As you color in the stripes and draw the stars discuss:

Why are there 50 stars in our flag? (A star for each of the 50 states.)

Why are there 13 red and white stripes? (There were 13 original colonies.)

What do the red stripes stand for? (Red for courage.)

What do the white stripes stand for? (White for freedom.)

What does the blue field stand for? (Blue for loyalty.)

What is loyalty? (It means being faithful and true; to show you care about something.)

What are some ways to show loyalty to the United States? (To really mean it when we pledge allegiance to the flag; to vote; to live in peace; to pray for our country; to respect all people.)

Puzzle Fun

The Fourth of July is a great time to help your children get better acquainted with their country.

At a variety or toy store buy a United States map puzzle. Work together and have fun putting the puzzle together. Then, locate your town, your part of the United States. Take 10 minutes to discover:

1. What is the name of your state?
2. What states surround your state?
3. Do you live nearest to the Atlantic or the Pacific Ocean?
4. Are you nearer to Canada or to Mexico?
5. In which part of the United States are you nearest to God?

Talk for a few minutes about how good it is to know God is with us wherever we are (see Joshua 1:9).

Write a Letter to the President

Read together Romans 13:1-7. *(The Living Bible* paraphrase is very clear.) Look especially at verse 7 and talk about how your family can "... give honor and respect to all those to whom it is due." Then work together to write a letter to the President.

Tell him of your family's prayers and support. (Take dictation from young children who can't print or write yet.) Don't worry about perfect wording or getting it all typed up "nice and neat." Father can enclose a note explaining how the letter was written by the family as a special way of doing something to honor the government and its leaders. Seal the letter in an envelope and address it to:

The President of the United States
The White House
Washington, D.C. 20500

Then pray together for the President and for all officials in high office. Pray especially for those who make a profession of faith in Christ. Ask God to give them wisdom for their very difficult tasks and to bless their families.

Summer Is the Time for Fun

by Jennie Douglas

I cannot truthfully say I am the type of mother who is at her best during the summer months. On the contrary, the middle of June to me has always signaled the advent of damp, wadded towels, wet bathing suits, open refrigerator doors, and the eternal, "Mama, what can we do now?" It always seems that school is out forever and I am completely bored by hotdogs and potato salad long before the end of July.

Last June, the day after school was out, I was desultorily watering the lawn and feeling sorry for myself when my neighbor across the street emerged from her house. She and her three children were all dressed up and I crossed the street to admire her new plaid seersucker suit. "We're going out for a celebration lunch," she said gaily while the kids beamed.

"Somebody's birthday?" I asked.

"Oh, no. We're celebrating because school's out."

I didn't say anything, but my face must have spoken for me because she immediately went on, "The kids and I hardly see each other except at meals during the school year what with Scouts, Little League, homework and piano lessons; and I'm always busy with my church work and P.T.A. I just let everything go during the summer and we go places together and get reacquainted."

I went back to my watering, very skeptical of the whole idea. But I mentioned it to my husband that night. He was

openly enthusiastic and eager to help with all sorts of ideas. The summer loomed even larger than most because we had been forced to forego our usual vacation due to unexpected dental and medical bills. My husband's enthusiasm was infectious.

Most of the outings we planned were free. We visited several factories, including a dairy which delighted the children by passing out ice cream at the end of the guided tour. We attended many of the city council meetings which met each Tuesday morning. The children, then 11 and 12, were fascinated; and I made a mental note not to vote for a certain councilman again after watching him in action a few times.

We also attended several court sessions. All of us were spellbound. No TV courtroom drama will ever satisfy us after our taste of the real thing. It sparked marvelous family discussions each evening too. Instead of the customary, "What did you do today, Tony?" and the usual answer, "Aw, nothing much, just messed around," we were debating the broad questions of inheritance laws, divorce, the causes of crime and the effectiveness of the entire judicial system.

I had always left the back-to-school shopping until August, usually running up a dress or two for Laura and a shirt for Tony for the first day of school. This year Laura and I planned to sew everything and bought the material in one fell swoop. We purchased orange colored, wash-and-wear gabardine for a skirt, pants and a jacket; a brown, orange and white geometric print for a matching blouse and skirt, brown corduroy for extra pants and two remnants for blouses—one beige with tiny brown flowers and the other a striped silk in shades of green. We worked together slowly, talking as we pinned and stitched. At first Laura did

only the easy parts—long, straight seams, darts and hems—but during August she cut out and sewed the corduroy pants all by herself. Best of all, she kept right on sewing after school began.

We visited our county museum and were fortunate enough to see a special exhibit of Dorothea Lange's poignant pictures of the depression years. We had to stop on the way home to buy film for Tony's camera, and, from then on, he took pictures wherever we went. His father had once been very interested in photography and the two of them finally located the box in the garage that contained his old darkroom equipment. Since then they have spent a great deal of time together, happily dealing with negatives and hypo.

I had always read aloud to the children in the evening. Now we switched to after lunch and were sometimes so enthralled that we read the afternoon away. It took us a long time to get through *No Time for Sergeants* because we spent half the time laughing, but we finished it, as well as *Born Free* and *Cheaper by the Dozen,* by the end of the summer.

Formerly I had dropped the children with their friends at the beach several times a week, making arrangements for another mother to pick them up later. Now the three of us went together. We would arrive promptly at 9 A.M. when the lifeguard went on duty. Two hours later when the beach became crowded, we would leave. We would hurry home for quick showers and then tackle the housework.

Laura ran the clothes through the washer and dryer and did the dishes, while Tony made the beds and I dusted and vacuumed. Strangely enough, the children never complained about helping with the housework and they often helped me prepare dinner, too. I did notice that Tony wasn't quite as keen about "Chicken Kiev" after he had

had a turn at boning and pounding the chicken breasts. This aspect of summer paid an unexpected dividend the following January when I had the "flu" and the two children managed to cook dinner for their father three nights in a row.

Summer was almost over before I realized it. It was with quite an uncharacteristic pang of regret that I watched the children go off to school in September. We had all had the best summer ever and we *were* better acquainted. We had a vast store of shared experiences and conversations which proved deeply rewarding to us. The happenings of the summer continued to influence us during the school year. Dinner table conversation was far more fluent and voluble. I noticed that the children squabbled less than formerly and TV watching decreased considerably.

Now we are making plans for next summer. We have decided to skip our vacation again this year and save the money for an extended trip to Mexico the following summer. With this in mind, we have enrolled the whole family for an early evening class in conversational Spanish. We plan to practice with each other and do our homework together. We are anxious to resume our visits to the city council chambers and the courtroom. And we also have an ambitious money-saving summer scheme. I have never canned any food before but we plan to take advantage of the low, summer fruit prices and put away some fruit for the winter and make jam, too. The children have a passion for dill pickles and we will try our hand at those as well.

The very first thing we plan to do, however, is to dress up and go out for a celebration lunch the first day after school's out. All of us are agreed that summer's the time for fun.

—From *Family Digest*. Copyright 1974 by Our Sunday Visitor, Inc., Huntington, Indiana 46750. Used by permission.

Summer Bible Learning Adventures

by Gwen Fodge

Summer's long days and relaxed schedules provide special opportunities for you to share God's Word with your family. Whether you are vacationing or spending these last weeks of summer at home, be alert for appropriate moments to talk with your family about God's love and His Word.

• Are you spending time at the beach? Take time to read Matthew 7:24-27 with your family. Then when the tide is out build a sand castle below the high tide line. Beside your sand castle pile a few heavy rocks. Then watch what happens when the tide comes in. (The sand castle washes away but the rocks stay put.) Share ideas on how this illustrates Jesus' story. Help your children identify Jesus as "the Rock." Let them know that you trust Him because He is dependable; a safe foundation for life.

• Because summer is a time of planting and watching things grow you have good opportunities to talk about Christian growth. Sprout bean seeds between warm, damp paper towels to illustrate 1 Peter 2:2. Or, there is still time this summer to plant radishes. (They grow fast!) As your children watch the plants grow share thoughts on how we grow as Christians. For ideas read Ephesians 4:15; 1 Thessalonians 3:12; 2 Peter 3:18.

• A rainy day doesn't have to be a disaster. Provide materials so your children can make simple puppets. Old socks or brown paper bags, colored paper, paste and crayons are good puppet makings. Encourage your youngsters to put together a Bible story puppet show to present to the family after dinner.

• If your child brings you a hand-picked bouquet, put the flowers on the dinner table and let your devotions center on them. Read Matthew 6:28-34; talk about how God makes beautiful things and how He cares for all of His creation. Flowers remind us that God cares for us and promises to provide our needs.

• This summer choose an exciting true adventure story about a Christian—perhaps a famous personality, a missionary or an athlete—and read it aloud, one chapter at a time. Plan to read when the family can relax and enjoy the story together. Look for ways God's Word had an effect on the person's life. Suggestion: If you have teenagers or older children read together *Prodigal Father,* Heath Bottomly (Regal Books)—the exciting story of a command fighter pilot who discovers peace.

• Young children enjoy acting out Bible stories. Help your children (and possibly their visiting friends) choose the story, name the characters and decide who will take each part. Make sure everyone has a part. In Daniel and the lion's den, for example, you'll need Daniel, the king, and at least one lion. For more "actors" add more lions, one or more guards or scoffing onlookers. The children may enjoy preparing simple costumes—a paper crown for the king, a yarn tail for the lion. Mother and Dad should take part—children love it when parents join in.

Celebrate Good Times Together

The following family time activities will give you ideas for ways your family can have good times together during the summer.

Plan a Show-and-Tell Time

One of the great things about being God's child is that we can enjoy being who we are (no need to pretend we're someone else). We can have fun doing what we can do because we recognize "God has given each of us the ability to do certain things..." (Rom. 12:6, *The Living Bible*).

Help your family experience the reality of these truths by planning a Show-and-Tell evening.

Plan your Show-and-Tell evening a week in advance so each family member can prepare something to share. Remember, not all accomplishments result in a finished product. Perhaps learning to swim, or learning to ride his two-wheeler or mastering a skateboard or learning to play "Chopsticks" is the highlight of your child's year. Suggest he plan to give a demonstration to the family.

Perhaps Dad will want to show some old family movies or slides. Mom may have an interest or hobby to share.

Other possibilities include showing things you have collected, telling about funny happenings or interesting things you've seen, even sharing a favorite riddle or joke. Perhaps someone has drawings to show or will want to read a poem he has written.

While some children can take one of these (or similar) ideas and put it into action, other children need a bit of thoughtful guidance. Questions are perhaps the best way to help a child think through a process. "Brad, what do you like to do best? What have you done of which you're most proud?"

Also, offer clues as to available materials with which he can work. "There's a dandy board in the garage that you might use to display and label your rock collection." (Do NOT insist they follow your suggestions.)

The secret to the success of your Show-and-Tell evening is for everyone to listen to the other person. Mom and Dad need to model "active listening" —really thinking about what a person is saying rather than letting your thoughts race ahead to what YOU'RE going to say next. As you "active listen" ask questions to reflect what the person has said. "Brad, you seem to be saying that these rocks containing veins of metal are the most interesting to you. Where would be a place you'd like to go hunting for these kinds of rocks?" This demonstration of your interest helps Brad feel you really value the things that interest him.

After Show-and-Tell, take a few minutes to point out that it makes your family more fun because each member has different interests and talents. Share a prayer of thanksgiving for the different talents and abilities God has given each member of your family. Thank God for each one by name.

Good Morning, Lord

Plan an early morning summer adventure. It can be a hike, with a trail-foods breakfast; a cookout in a nearby park; a brisk walk around your block. Whatever you plan, have everything ready the evening before and set the alarm so your family can experience the early morning air.

As you go out into the morning light, talk about what makes morning come and the darkness of night leave. Talk about the sun, the source of light God created for day. Feel the sun's warmth. Notice how much cooler it is when you are in the shade.

When you get to your destination, make a game of "listening to the morning." Any birds singing? Any breeze blowing? Any roosters crowing? Any dogs barking?

Before you eat, take a few minutes for "nature snooping." Can everyone discover five different living things? Plants or bugs or... What can *you* find?

As you eat, talk about what you like best about getting out into the early morning. Part of the family may have complaints; listen to them too, and promise sleep-in time the following day.

After breakfast, while the family is still gathered together, take three cards from your pocket on which you've lettered (one verse on each card) Colossians 1:15-17 from *The Living Bible* paraphrase. Have three members of the family read the verses and then talk together to see who can remember *three* important things these verses say about Jesus. (The verses may have to be read a number of times to help the family come up with: *Jesus is exactly like God; Jesus—God Himself—created everything in heaven and earth; and it is Jesus who holds everything together.*)

Encourage everyone to look around. Light, trees, sunshine, birds—everything is part of what Jesus the Creator planned and made.

Nature Poster

Wherever you are for your morning adventure (beach or campsite, or a field on a farm) work as a family. First, smooth a piece of ground or choose a plot of grass for a background where you can make a nature poster. Then, using rocks, twigs, leaves and whatever you can find, letter the words, "His power holds everything together," from Colossians 1:17 (see Fig. 15).

Before you make the poster agree to use only things of nature you find on the ground. Do not break or hurt plants, bushes or trees. As you work, get everyone's idea on different ways Jesus holds His creation together: stars and planets in dependable orbits; day and night without fail; plants that grow seeds that grow more plants that provide food; tides that rise and fall twice every day, and waves that never cease beating against the shore; gravity that holds things in their place and keeps them from falling from the earth.

Fig. 15

Celebrate Easter— Jesus Is Alive!

The Good Friday Reading

by Frieda Barkman

During Lent our family reads the Gospel according to Matthew, Mark, Luke or John, whichever the children choose. During Passion Week we follow the reading for each day,* a custom established even before the children graduated from their first Bible storybook.

But when did spiritual significance attach itself to our ritual? Was it when John, then a first-grader, jumped eagerly into my lap with his open-at-Matthew Bible and urged, "Read it to me again. Mommie, *please*, from the beginning!"?

*See Matthew 21—28:2

He was able to follow the words, being in his third primer at school, and so, as requested, I turned back the pages of Matthew to Palm Sunday. The past became the present as we once again marched in the parade. Jesus rides on a little donkey and everybody crowds near to carpet the road with their wraps. Those who can reach, cut branches to spread in His path. (Palm branches, likely, that's why it's called Palm Sunday.) Everyone raises his voice and shouts, "Hosanna! Praise Him, praise Him, blessings on Him who comes in the name of the Lord."

We follow our Lord. Now He is in the Temple, which resembles a crowded shopping center. There is much noise of bargaining and selling. Jesus upsets the money-changers' tables: crates tumble and pigeons flutter everywhere. We hear Jesus' strong voice vibrating across the court. "My house shall be a house of prayer. You are making it a hideout for thieves."

The next moment Jesus turns from the crowd and touches a blind man and heals a crippled man crouched in the corner. The boys in the Temple watch Him and shout again, "Hosanna!" (Sort of like, "Look what Jesus did!")

But the leaders are mad and indignant, and they're out to trap Jesus. We hold our breath as Jesus answers their trick questions. We know they are evil men looking for a chance to arrest Him and put Him to death.

Next we notice Judas speaking to the high priest and we can't believe what we hear. He's going to hand Jesus over to the enemy for 30 pieces of silver. *No, Judas!*

Then we climb the stone steps at night—and they're steep!—to a friend's upstairs room. Jesus is eating His last supper with His friends. We hear the men sing a hymn and watch them walk quietly out into the night.

We walk with them in the white moonlight to the garden. Jesus goes to pray but the disciples are so tired they fall asleep on the grass. Three times Jesus prays alone while they sleep.

Was it just another story, I wondered, as my son sat contemplative and unmoving. Or was his soul ready to emerge? Was John ready to make contact with his God? Were we on the verge of a new understanding of Jesus and His suffering?

It was a time similar to that first knowing oneness that passed between us, mother and child, when he was just a few weeks old and gave me that first smile of recognition. I held him then, loved him, but knew my arms and my love would someday not be enough. Someday I would want my child to respond to God in the same way—a smile, a seal of knowing and belonging.

And so from the day John was big enough to sleep in his own bed, I read to him about God and hung a motto on his door, "Grant to little children visions bright of Thee." Closing his door, I invariably gave those words a silent glance, as if God needed reminding to send those visions bright.

Day after month after year, and now John seemed so quietly knowing as he sat there on my lap and I continued the Passion story.

A noise jolts us as the Temple police arrive with swords and cudgels to arrest Jesus. Yes, there's Judas kissing Jesus to identify Him. We shudder as the soldiers grab Him.

We hear the priests, lawyers and elders arguing about the charges. Tensions mount as they spit in His face and strike Him with their fists. Consultations and cursing continue all night. Toward morning a rooster crows and Peter goes out crying.

With clanging chains they bind Jesus and lead Him to the governor where the trial continues. More questions. Mobs begin shouting, "Crucify Him!"

Pilate's soldiers yank off Jesus' clothes, throw a purple robe on Him and push long thorns deep into His head for a crown. They beat Him about the head with a cane and spit on Him—"King! King!"

And then they lead Him away to be crucified.

John sat motionless, the only sound was a sigh. We had finished the repeat and come to the place of today's reading. Good Friday.

"Read all of it, Mommie," he ordered. "Don't skip anything." We had omitted some long discourses earlier. Had he sensed my hesitancy? Should I read it all? I just wasn't sure.

My heart wanted to shrink from the nails, the scourging, the stabbing. Shouldn't I shield my child from such cruelty and hate? I questioned. Surely, for a tender six-year-old, such an encounter would leave a scar. Yet, "He was wounded for our transgressions"* and the story of hate has its counterpart of love, deepest, highest love! Still I pondered, can a child understand love?

I decided to read it all. After all, it was the greatest point of history, the pivotal point of Christianity. I would "tell it like it is." I knew the concepts of redemption from sin and eternal life might be too deep for a six-year-old, but no one is too young to understand love. The fuller concepts will grow with him.

My son's impatience outran my deliberations.

"Read all of it," he repeated softly and emphatically as he resettled himself on my lap. So, together we went to the cross.

It is a heavy wooden cross that Jesus carries—so heavy that He falls and Simon has to help Him carry it partway up the cruel hill. We cringe as the soldiers pound the nails through His hands and feet. We see them toss dice for His

*Isaiah 53:5 (KJV)

seamless tunic. Some soldier will probably wear it strutting down a Jerusalem street later that afternoon. We hear the bandit taunt Him, while the other one asks for help and receives a prompt promise of paradise from Jesus' lips.

We stand close to the beloved disciple (his name is John, too), and we hear women weeping. Jesus' mother leans on John's strong arm. With the help of Mark, Luke and John we follow Jesus' seven last words and hear His last cry. At three o'clock the earth trembles—Jesus dies and is buried.

A tear (was it John's or mine?) tumbles big on the page, wrinkling the India paper. We brush it off as we are caught in the darkness of midday.

The Good Friday reading was ended. The silence was heavy. But could I really stop there? No, I was sure I couldn't leave my son there. All the shock of Good Friday—the cross, the death, the tomb—had a sequel, and John had to know about it. I read on.

"The Sabbath had passed, and it was about daybreak on Sunday when—"

"Mommie!" John cried in reprimand, "that's for the day after tomorrow." And then in a whisper, "But we already know, don't we?"

Only an India paper thickness between death and life. Did he really know?

Today (those six tender years have more than doubled), I asked him, "John, when did the cross take on meaning for you? When did Jesus become your Saviour?"

"In the other house, alone in my bedroom. Only I did it several times to make sure," he volunteered.

We lived in the "other house" when he was six and we read together at Eastertime.

—Adapted from *Look for the Wonder* (Regal Books, 1975).

Why Did Jesus Have to Die?

by Margaret Self

Long before a little child can comprehend the full meaning of "Jesus Is Risen!" he can sense that Easter is a joyful day.

A child likes the gay colors, the happy songs, the beautiful flowers and expressions of love and kindness that are part of the wonderful Christian festival we call Easter. And he will reflect the attitudes and actions of those adults around him who love Jesus and give thanks because He lives. Your feelings of joy will communicate even to your very young child that Easter is a happy time.

But as a child's ability to understand increases so does his curiosity, and as he wonders, he asks...why?...who? ...what? Here are several questions your child may ask as he hears about the first Easter. The following suggestions will help you give meaningful answers he can accept and understand.

Why did they kill Jesus?

Jesus was hurt and killed by men who did not like Him. They did not know that God sent the Lord Jesus to love and help everyone. But God made Jesus alive again. Jesus is living! (Matt. 27:22-26).

Where is Jesus?

He is living in heaven now. We do not know exactly where heaven is, but God is there. The Lord Jesus is there. Everything is very, very beautiful in heaven. And everyone is very, very happy there (Eph. 1:20; Col. 3:1).

What is Jesus doing in heaven?

Jesus told us He is making a wonderful home in heaven. All who love Him (everyone in God's family) will be with Him in heaven someday (John 14:1-7).

What is it like in heaven?

The Bible tells us that it is more beautiful than we can ever think. No one gets sick or hurt there. There is no sadness—only happiness! No tears—only happy faces and singing voices (Rev. 21; 22).

Will the Lord Jesus come again to this earth?

Yes! But only the Lord God knows when it will be ...some wonderful, wonderful day! Everyone who loves the Lord Jesus (everyone in God's family) will be glad to see Him and to go with Him to the heavenly home He has made (1 Thess. 4:14—5:10; Acts 1:9-11).

Easter Is a Happy Time!

by Wes Haystead

Four-year-old Alan thought he had Easter analyzed. Confidently he explained: "It was when Jesus arose from the grave and the Easter bunny hopped out after Him!"

Easter is a joyful time, but it can also be a time of confusion for children as they get the secular and biblical aspects of the Easter celebration confused. Easter baskets, eggs and bunnies sometimes overshadow the true and beautiful Easter story from God's Word.

"We are happy at Easter because Jesus is alive!" is what your child needs to hear from you often at Eastertime. Spring flowers, happy music, brightly colored eggs, gifts, even new clothes can all be made a meaningful part of your Easter celebration when children are helped to understand that all of these things can be used by people to show and share their joy because *Jesus is living*.

The biblical truth that *Jesus is alive* is what your child needs to remember long after Easter day is past.

Parents need to keep in mind that words and phrases that are quite clear to adults often have clouded meanings for young children. For example, "Jesus died and rose again" is not likely to have meaning or seem like a happy statement to little children.

Children have very vague and uneasy notions about what death involves. They usually see it as some kind of sad separation.

Instead of dwelling on the details of Christ's death, help your child grasp the great truth of the Easter story—a living Saviour. You can help him understand by talking about the way Jesus' friends must have felt:

"Jesus' friends were very sad when Jesus died. Some of them even cried because they thought they would never see Jesus again. You can imagine how very happy they were when they found out that Jesus did not stay dead! They must have laughed and hugged each other and told all of their friends, 'Jesus isn't dead. He is alive! Jesus is living.' "

Tell the simple facts of the Crucifixion story, but for the young child, avoid dwelling on the gruesome aspects that may emotionally overwhelm him.

After you talk about the first Easter, take time to encourage your youngster to draw a picture story of Easter. Talking with him about his art will give you opportunities to observe what was most important to him, clarify any misconceptions he has and to build happy feelings about the Easter story.

—Adapted from *You Can't Begin Too Soon,* Wes Haystead (Regal Books, 1975). Used by permission.

A poem with motions your young child will enjoy...

The First Easter

Mary walked to the garden

She looked all around

But her dear friend Jesus

Could nowhere be found.

As Mary was turning

A kind voice she heard

"Mary!" the man said,

And it was the Lord.

Oh, Mary was happy!

She ran all the way

To tell "Jesus is living,"

That first Easter day.

Judith B. Kaiser

A Lenten Journey of Love

Traditionally, the six weeks before Easter is a time called Lent—a time of remembering Christ's love and His giving of Himself for us. These weeks can have special meaning for your family if you make Lent a time of praising God for His love and planning ways to share His love with others.

Dr. James C. Pippin, a pastor in Oklahoma, originated a Lenten "Journey of Love" for use during the weeks before Easter.

Early in Lent go over the "Journey of Love" with your family. Talk about ways your family can use the suggested activities and reach out to others with Christlike love. Together read Paul's words, "Each of you should look not only to your own interests, but also to the interests of others. Your attitude should be the same as that of Christ Jesus: who...humbled himself and became obedient to death—even death on a cross" (Phil. 2:4-8, *NIV*).

First Week: The Hand of Love. Write a letter a day to a friend, near or far away. Tell someone how much you appreciate him or her.

Second Week: The Voice of Love. Telephone two or three people each day for a short chat to say what they mean to you or to say "Thank you" or "I'm sorry." Call

people you have intended to phone but somehow never have.

Third Week: The Deed of Love. Take a gift—something you have made or bought—to two or three friends who mean much to you. It can be simple—fruit, cookies, a plant—some small remembrance that has love as a wrapping.

Fourth Week: The Heart of Love. Make a list of at least 10 people for whom you will pray daily. (Maybe members of your family will want to divide the list.) Include on the list your friends, your enemies, those you don't like. Forgive them if they have wronged you, and ask forgiveness if you have wronged them.

Fifth Week: The Mind of Love. Use this week to pray for yourself and to look inward. Praise God for His love. At church meditate on the meaning of Easter as you worship with joy.

Sixth Week: The Victory of Love. This is the week of celebration. Thank God for His love revealed in many ways. Rejoice that Christ lives. Get out-of-doors and breathe in the air of spring. Let your joy be full with life abundant in faith, hope and love. Praise God!

Bible
Readings for Lent

During the weeks before Easter, read Bible portions that help your family learn more about Jesus—His great power and how He showed that He really loved people and cared about their needs. Your family can enjoy making a sketchbook by drawing pictures that illustrate these incidents from Jesus' life. Include drawings by every member of the family. Next Eastertime your sketchbook will be a family treasure.

Read about Jesus...
  Loves the children—Mark 10:13-16
  Heals a sick woman—Mark 1:29-31
  Makes a child well—Mark 5:22,23,35-42
  Forgives and heals—Luke 5:17-26
  Blesses Simon Peter with many fish—Luke 5:4-9
  Feeds 5,000 with just a little food—Mark 6:30-44
  Heals a deaf man—Mark 7:32-37
  Stills the storm—Matthew 8:23-27
  Heals a blind man—Mark 10:46-52
  Heals 10 lepers—Luke 17:11-19
  Walks on the water—Matthew 14:22-32
  Tells His friends that He is the way to God—
      John 14:1-6
  Dies for our sins—Matthew 27:27-60
  Lives again—Luke 24:1-32; John 20:11-18
  Returns to heaven and promises to come to earth
      again—Luke 24:38-53; John 14:1-6

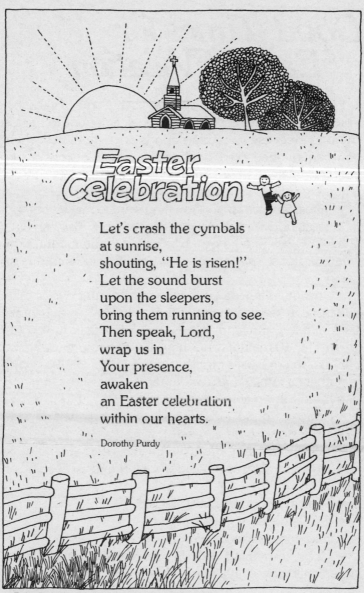

Easter Celebration

Let's crash the cymbals
at sunrise,
shouting, "He is risen!"
Let the sound burst
upon the sleepers,
bring them running to see.
Then speak, Lord,
wrap us in
Your presence,
awaken
an Easter celebration
within our hearts.

Dorothy Purdy

—From *Decision* (copyright 1972). Used by permission.

Good Times for Easter Vacation

For many families "Easter week" is that time of vacation from school for the children, the week just prior to Easter Sunday. Because vacation periods are oftentimes when you want or need extra ideas for things to do, we're giving you several suggestions for things to make, places to go and things to do.

● Take a trip as a family. You may want to make your trip a "one-day drive" to a predetermined spot. You can also make it a walk, a hike or a bike ride. Decide together on what kind of a "trip" you think your family would most enjoy.

● One intriguing idea is to take a half-hour drive or bike ride using a "destination unknown coin flip" at each intersection. If the coin lands heads, turn left; if tails, turn right. Try this for 30 minutes and then stop to explore (or figure out how to get back home!).

● Invite a family over for dinner.

● Read a story aloud.

● Choose a good TV special to enjoy together.

● Tell a story about yourself.

● Talk about memories from Easters past.

● Invite grandparents over for supper and an evening of visiting.

● Look at old photos and slides.

● Visit a museum, park or library.

● Hike someplace an hour away.

● Cook something as a family project. Some gather ingredients. Some measure. Others mix. Everyone laughs and eats!

• Make a list of family blessings. Write God a letter of thanks.

• Color Easter eggs the old-fashioned Pennsylvania Dutch way—with dry onion hulls. Place a generous heap of dry onionskins in a large kettle, add cold water and carefully place uncooked eggs in the onionskin and water mixture. Cook slowly over a low flame until eggs are hard-boiled. You'll be delighted to find the eggs have turned a beautiful rusty brown.

• Plan an Easter egg hunt. Why eggs at Easter? Throughout the centuries the egg has been used at Easter as a symbol of new life, a reminder of God's power. A chick breaking free from the egg's shell is one of the wonders of God's creation!

• Use the following "make and do" activities to help your family think and talk about the true meaning of Easter. Especially, take time to work on the Easter Story Frieze even if your family isn't too artistic. Involving your children in drawing the pictures and taping them together will help them remember the sequence of events in the Easter story.

Create an Easter Story Frieze

Get out crayons and sheets of paper and work together to create an Easter story frieze. (A frieze is a series of pictures that tell a story.)

Give each family member a generous piece of paper on which to draw his part of the story. Then, when everyone has finished, tape the pictures together. (Let everyone draw in the way that is most comfortable to him. "Style" of art need not match!)

Pictures that your family may want to include in your Easter story frieze are: Jesus riding into Jerusalem on a donkey (Palm Sunday); Jesus eating with His disciples

Fig. 16

(The Last Supper); Jesus being captured in the garden; Jesus before Pilate; Jesus being crucified; and then... The Empty Tomb! (See Fig. 16.)

Help your family get ideas for each picture by reading the Easter story from Matthew 28:1-9 or Mark 16:1-7.

Nail Art for Easter

Your older children can create a good-looking Christian symbol plaque with very little help. (See Fig. 17.) Explain that the fish sign is a symbol that has been used to identify Christians from the time of the early Church until now.

To make the plaque, your children will need a 4x6-inch piece of wood approximately 1½ to 2-inches thick; 1½-inch finishing nails; hammer; stain; varnish; brush; a file or chisel; pencil; brass hanger.

Cut a symbol pattern (cross or fish) from paper. Trace around pattern on lightweight cardboard and cut out.

Give wood a "distressed" look by leaving the edges and sides rough. Add a few nicks and gouges with hammer, file or chisel. Stain top and sides of wood. Let dry. Varnish wood. Let dry. Use pattern to trace design on wood. Hammer the nails into the design outline about ⅛-inch apart. Leave about ½-inch of nail above the surface. Hammer nails as straight as possible.

Think about this: Can a plaque on the wall be a witness? How? How can a simple plaque help you celebrate Easter?

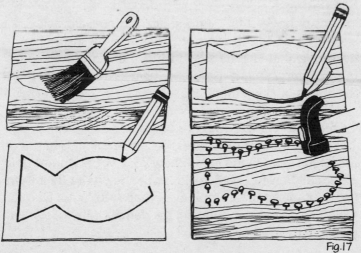

Fig.17

Family Celebration of the Resurrection

Which would work best at your house—an Easter eve celebration, looking forward to Easter morning? Or a family Easter sunrise celebration (before you get ready for church)?

Talk together and decide what your family wants to do, then begin to plan. Encourage everyone to contribute his ideas and make certain each person in the family has an opportunity to participate in the celebration. The important thing is to keep your celebration simple, happy and meaningful for your group. Here are a few suggestions.

Sing Songs

"Jesus Loves Me" sung softly, remembering Jesus is alive, can be a true song of praise and an inspiration to everyone in the family. Also include familiar Easter songs. For accompaniment use guitar, piano, simple rhythm instruments or clapping hands.

Create Your Own Easter Litany

The following litany (or responsive reading) is based on the Easter story found in Matthew 28:1-9. Encourage your older children to use it for ideas as they write their own. (When their litany is complete, perhaps Mother or Dad can type copies so everyone in the family can follow and respond.)

JESUS CHRIST IS RISEN

Reader: The angel said to the women, "Do not be afraid, for I know you are looking for Jesus, who was crucified."

All: We are looking for Jesus.

Reader: He is not here; He is risen just as He said. Come and see the place where He lay.

All: We are coming to look where Jesus lay. We are looking and He is gone! We cannot see Jesus!

Reader: He is risen from the dead. Jesus Christ is risen!

All: He is risen indeed!

Reader: Jesus Christ is risen!

All: He is risen indeed!

Reader: Jesus Christ our Saviour is risen! Thank you, God, that Jesus is alive.

All: Our Saviour Jesus is risen. Thank you, Jesus, we are glad, you are alive. We are glad you are alive!

Note: Your family may prefer to read the Easter story responsively from one of the Gospels. Let your children decide which Bible account they want to use by reading each one before your family celebration.

Include praise and prayer in your Resurrection celebration. Thank God for Jesus. Thank Jesus for all He did.

Make an Easter Celebration Banner

For creative and meaningful family fun, design and construct an Easter Celebration Banner.

Begin by planning together and making a sketch of how you want your banner to look. For ideas, look at Figure 18, but then go on to incorporate your own ideas. Make sure to include items or symbols of the important events in Jesus' last week before His death and resurrection. For example, a palm branch, a loaf of bread and a cup, a crown of thorns, a cross, an empty tomb.

Gather the material you will need: a piece of burlap

2½x4 feet (or even 3x5 feet if you want a really big banner). You'll also need scissors, newspapers, glue, colored felt, bright yarn—and whatever other decorations you want to include.

Now, everyone join in making the banner. First, hem the top edge of the burlap and insert a dowel rod for rigidity. Fringe the side and bottom edges by pulling several threads.

Next, pencil an Easter phrase of praise on the burlap. Then working with glue and yarn, "write" each word.

You can cut letters and symbols from brightly-colored felt squares (available at most yardage stores). Note: before you cut the letters and symbols from the felt, experiment

Fig. 18

with cutting the shapes from sheets of newspaper until you come up with the exact shape you want. Then use the newspaper pattern for a guide.

Remember as you work on the banner to have fun. If a symbol is glued on a little crooked—fine. Working together is the real joy—not perfection.

When you have completed the banner, hang it in a prominent place where everyone can enjoy it. Then when Easter is over, pack it away for next year.

Make an Easter Candle

Use a large, thick white candle. Decorate two sides of the candle to give it special meaning for Easter.

Pin sequins on one side to form the shape of a cross. Or, instead of sequins punch whole cloves into the candle. (See Fig. 19.) Turn the candle and decorate the other side with sequins or cloves to form the word JOY.

Fig. 19

Make "I Remember" Crosses

Gather a variety of materials (twigs, small pieces of wood, heavy paper, bright pieces of yarn and colorful construction paper) from which each member of the family can make an "I Remember" cross to use in your Easter family time.

Fig. 20

Show everyone the sketches of crosses (Fig. 20), then encourage each person to design his own cross. Explain that all of the crosses will be used on Easter Day when the family gathers to thank Jesus for His great love.

For Easter Day—
A Time of Darkness, a Time of Light

Choose a time when the family will not be hurried—perhaps Easter late afternoon or early evening—for a quiet time using the "I Remember" crosses and the Easter candle your family prepared.

Place the unlighted Easter candle on a table so everyone can see the cross design. Comment: *Jesus died on the cross to take the punishment for our sins. Because He died we can ask God for forgiveness and become members of His family. We feel sad when we think about how much Jesus suffered for us. It was a sad, dark day for Jesus' friends when He died.*

Invite everyone to bring the cross he or she made and lay it on the table near the candle as a way of saying: "Jesus, I remember what you did for me and I thank you."

After the crosses are on the table, continue to comment: *Jesus' death was just the beginning of what happened on the first Easter...*

Remember and talk together about things that happened that first Easter morning. Comment that *the first Easter was a bright happy day—a time of great joy!*

Then turn the Easter candle so everyone can see the word JOY. Light the candle. Gather round and sing the songs you learned for Easter.

If you have a record of "The Hallelujah Chorus" from Handel's *Messiah,* play it. Begin softly as you explain that Hallelujah is a word like "how wonderful"—a glad, joyful word. Gradually increase the volume. Encourage everyone to join in and sing the Hallelujahs! Have a blessed Easter Day.

Jesus as Saviour and Lord

With all of the discussion this month about Christ dying for our sins, take advantage of the many natural opportunities that may arise to talk with your children about their personal salvation.

Make these points, simply and without pressuring your child:

1. God loves us and wants us to be part of His special family—those who believe in Jesus (1 John 4:8).

2. We have all done wrong things in our lives like stealing, cheating, lying and not believing in Jesus. The Bible calls these things sin (Rom. 3:23).

3. God loves us so much—He loves YOU so much—that He sent His Son, Jesus Christ, to die on the cross for your sin (1 Cor. 15:3).

4. If you are sorry for your sin, tell God right now that you are sorry. If you believe that Jesus died to be your Saviour, tell God that too. If you are really sorry for your sin and really believe in Jesus, God forgives all your sin. Now you are in God's special family (John 1:12) and you have God's gift of everlasting life. This means God is with you now and forever (John 3:16).

Celebrate with Thanksgiving

Thank You, Lord, for Peanut Butter

Couldn't I just have a peanut butter sandwich?

by Frieda Barkman

When, finally, I rang the old copper cowbell calling kith and kin to the table, the spread never looked more lavish. Holding hands for the traditional prayer of thanksgiving, a warmth quite unlike the oven heat of the previous hour enveloped me. Before I could identify the feeling, the bustle of Grandma snapping documentary pictures and the aroma urging us on to the carving, took precedence.

Then John, in a narrow parenthesis of silence asked, "Couldn't I just have a peanut butter sandwich?"

John is no connoisseur of exotic foods. His repertoire has always been slim, and the culinary arts are wasted on him, so he didn't surprise me. Wasn't he actually pointing us back to the basics of the first Thanksgiving Day?

The Pilgrims had wild bird, corn, and berries of the wood, venison maybe, but not famous English pot roast or spices of the Near East. They had starved and worked and some had died. And when they celebrated God's presence in the wilderness, it was for His provision of daily bread—the peanut butter sandwich.

Thanksgiving becomes the assurance that, "Thou preparest a table before me...Thou anointest my head with oil...I shall not want" (Ps. 23:5,1). It is a celebration of answered prayer, and as old as the Old Testament. It should be a festival of praise, joy, offerings and love.

Thanksgiving begins with words of praise.

Sometimes life becomes a problem instead of a privilege. We frequent God's complaint department and forget to praise. When it comes to the common courtesy of thanking God and others, we rate in the lower percentile.

With grumblings as common as bread and butter we begin each meal with thanks. Grace at the table becomes an indelible habit and food tastes bland without it. But the routine may become so commonplace that we subtly presume a legal right to our daily provisions. When the wonder and goodness of daily bread loses its nutritious aroma, "Many a blessing becomes stale because it is not renewed by thanksgiving."*

To put the flavor back into the bread I say "grace" as I walk in with the grocery bags. For the money spent, the bags may not be as heavy as they once were, but God gives health and strength to earn the money, and I give thanks for that.

Table grace is extended not only to grocery grace but to bank grace. As I post deposits I voice my own litany of thanks (inflation and taxes notwithstanding):

"...for our income that pays for food, education for the children, necessities, and the luxuries we think are necessities, thanks, Lord.

"...and for my husband, and for my children, thanks so much, Lord."

*John Henry Jowett, Daily Meditations, p. 230.

As I run the total and post the weekly deposit, the amen to my litany comes out in staccato like the adding machine. "A thousand times more good than we deserve, God gives us every day." And as always happens when we add up our thanks, joy begins to filter through.

Yet all His good gifts do not add up to joy. Only He does! When we love Him for Himself, not for all His good gifts, our cup begins to run over. Jesus is our joy.

A patient once said to my husband Paul, "People who have 'religion' seem to think it's so terrific. Is it really?"

In partial answer, Paul quoted from an anonymous Latin hymn of the eleventh century, "Jesus, Thou joy of loving hearts, from the best joy that earth imparts, we turn unfilled to Thee again."

The Latin version of joy is not so different from my common house variety. When Jesus walks into my kitchen He brings a gourmet recipe of joy. Thanksgiving is real joy.

It is giving too. Words are not enough. In our joy we must break off a corner of the gifts He has given us and return them to Him; a piece of the day we ought to return to Him; a part of our money we should put in the offering envelope and mail back to the Father.

Each year our family selects a Christmas project on Thanksgiving Day. A gold box receives our nickels, dimes, checks (our gold, frankincense and myrrh), which must exceed what we give to each other. Like King David we "will not offer burnt offerings to the Lord my God which cost me nothing" (2 Sam. 24:24). And our mental arithmetic on Christmas morning often tells us to write another check. What with bicycles, transistor radios, perfume, attaché case, we still don't give Him much more than a manger bed.

Thanksgiving is also loving. Lisa began a custom at our house. When a package announced a birthday or Christmas, she opened it, gasped, and then darted to Daddy and Mommie to plant a kiss. Her spontaneous thanks was better than saying thank you. Thanksgiving is giving a kiss. It is wrapping love around a person, like an embrace.

Too many of us lack this freedom to love. We have grown up in a staid, nondemonstrative culture. To shed a tear is a sign of weakness. We laugh about the apostle's instruction to "Greet one another with the kiss of love" (1 Pet. 5:14, NIV).

I came from such a non-embracing and non-kissing (except for babies) family, but I have since broken through our cultured pattern to a more honest display of emotions. Like others, I needed a new definition of love.

God is love. He is our source of supply. He wants to release His love through us. More than gifts, He wants us to give ourselves; to reach out and touch someone with kindness, warmth and openness; to share one another's hurts and burdens. This is keeping love for one another at full strength (see 1 Pet. 4:8). This new clasping, caring, touching as a rediscovery of the sacrament of the holy kiss is the symbol of love that has been limited too long to the realm of the physical.

Everyone needs this demonstrative love. Everyone needs someone to pray with, laugh with, cry with. I had this need. I dared to open up and expose myself at church one day. And someone put an arm around me and prayed for me, and gave me the holy kiss. Love was redefined. In turn I could begin to love others.

Giving praise to God is just words, but even so it starts a cycle. When we give Him praise, He gives us joy. Joy wants to give offerings, and does. To give ourselves is even better. That's love. That's thanksgiving.

—Adapted from *Look for the Wonder* (Regal Books, 1975).

Thanks Be to God

It is a good thing to give thanks unto the Lord, and to sing praises... Psalm 92:1

Thanksgiving Acrostic

Use this Thanksgiving Acrostic as a source of Scriptures for mealtime conversations during November. Share one of the Bible statements. Take time to talk about what it says and what it means to you. Get ideas from different family members about what each Bible quotation can mean in everyday life. Together thank God for His Word and His promises.

Thanks be to God for His indescribable gift! (2 Cor. 9:15, *NASB*).

Happy (is) the man who puts his trust in the Lord (Prov. 16:20, *TLB*).

And be sure of this—that I am with you always, even to the end of the world (Matt. 28:20, *TLB*).

Nor height, nor depth, nor any other created thing, shall be able to separate us from the love of God, which is in Christ Jesus our Lord (Rom. 8:39, *NASB*).

Know ye that the Lord he is God: it is he that hath made us, and not we ourselves; we are his people, and the sheep of his pasture (Ps. 100:3, *KJV*).

Shout joyfully to the Lord, all the earth. Serve the Lord with gladness; Come before Him with joyful singing (Ps. 100:1,2, *NASB*).

God is our refuge and strength, a very present help in trouble (Ps. 46:1, *NASB*).

If we confess our sins, He is faithful and righteous to forgive us our sins and to cleanse us from all unrighteousness (1 John 1:9, *NASB*).

Verily, verily, I say unto you, He that heareth my word, and believeth on him that sent me, hath everlasting life (John 5:24, *KJV*).

I am the resurrection, and the life; he who believes in Me shall live even if he dies (John 11:25, *NASB*).

Now may the Lord of peace Himself continually grant you peace in every circumstance. The Lord be with you all! (2 Thess. 3:16, *NASB*).

Great is the Lord, and greatly to be praised (1 Chron. 16:25, *NASB*).

A Thanksgiving Prayer

Create a Thanksgiving prayer that expresses your family's feelings to use on Thanksgiving Day.

For ideas read together Psalm 107:1-8; Psalm 136 and Psalm 146. Choose words and phrases from these Psalms to include in your prayer. Also encourage each member of the family to add his or her own thanks to God.

Prepare copies of the prayer so on Thanksgiving Day each person in the family can participate as you read the prayer and praise God together.

There's Enough

"Thank You, God,
for something of which
There's Enough...
He has enough love
to cover
all your past.
He has enough power
and wisdom
to help you meet every
present situation.
And He has enough light
to brighten your future
forever.

Live by that!
Live by His love
and His promise.

For all your days
There's Enough...
Thank You, God.

Harold Leestma

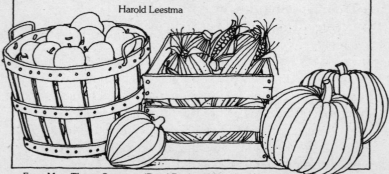

—From *More Than a Spectator* (Regal Books, 1974). Used by permission.

Children Prepare for Thanksgiving Day

Any celebration is more fun if everyone is involved in preparing for the special time. Use the following ideas—along with your own—and involve your children in preparing for Thanksgiving Day.

A Thanksgiving Puzzle Mural

You will need a 3x5-foot section of newsprint or butcher paper. Mark off two large jigsaw-puzzle type pieces for each family member (see Fig. 21). Put a small X on the front side of each piece (so all family members draw on the same side of the paper). Cut pieces apart and give each person two puzzle pieces to decorate with pictures and words. Here are some things family members might include on their sections:

• Something for which I am especially thankful this Thanksgiving.

• Something for which the Pilgrims were thankful on that first Thanksgiving.

• A Pilgrim, a church, a turkey, an Indian.

• Something for which I am not thankful but should be.

• A Scripture verse about giving thanks (1 Thess. 5:18; Phil. 4:6; Eph. 5:20; Ps. 92:1,2).

When puzzle pieces are complete, sprawl on the floor and put the puzzle back together (see Fig. 21). Tape it together and hang it on the wall. Let each person tell about his pieces of the puzzle. Praise God for His goodness.**

Fig. 21

Seed and Bean Mosaic

Autumn is harvesttime—a good time to make a seed or/and bean mosaic. Provide each child with lid from a margarine container, a variety of seeds (sunflower, etc.) and beans (split peas, pinto, navy, red beans, etc.). Let each child make his/her own design (see Fig. 22). The older members of the family will enjoy this activity too.

Making mosaics is a good way to keep children occupied and happy while the Thanksgiving meal is being prepared.

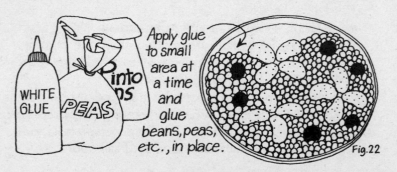

Apply glue to small area at a time and glue beans, peas, etc., in place.

WHITE GLUE

PEAS

Pinto ns

Fig. 22

Thanksgiving Place Mats

Materials: 12x18-inch piece of construction paper; small pieces of black, brown, white and orange paper; scissors, glue, drawing paper, pencil, paper napkin.

Procedure: Enlarge pilgrim outline to twice the size shown. Use this as a pattern to cut hat and tie from black paper; hair from brown, face from orange, and collar and buckle from white. Glue hat and face on place mat. Glue collar at top and side edges only. Add tie and buckle. Fold napkin and slip under collar (see Fig. 23).

Fig. 23

Thanksgiving Place Cards

Materials: One 5x6-inch piece of construction paper and Thanksgiving sticker for each place card.

Procedure: (Child completes a place card for each member of his family.) Fold construction paper in half lengthwise. Letter Psalm 136:1 and name of family member on it. Add sticker. (See Fig. 24.)

Fig. 24

2½"

6"

Cornucopia

Materials: A 9x9-inch piece of brown construction paper; stapler.

Procedure: Roll paper into a cone and staple. Cornucopia may be fastened to a piece of cardboard. Add real fruit, nuts and autumn leaves for a festive table decoration (see Fig. 25).

Fig. 25

A Game to Play on Thanksgiving Day

Draw a large turkey, minus the tail feathers, on a piece of butcher paper or poster board and attach it to the wall. Cut out a large turkey tail feather for each family member (see Fig. 26). Have each person draw a picture of something he is thankful for on the turkey tail feather and share it with the rest of the family. Then blindfold each family member, in turn, and have him pin or tape his tail feather on the turkey. This is special fun when simple prizes are given to the person closest to target... and the person farthest away.

Fig.26

Celebrate
Your Family
with Thanksgiving

These family time activities will help each person in your family think about how he appreciates the other members of the family and will give everyone opportunities to express appreciation to each family member.

Do you feel appreciated by others in your family? Do others in your family feel appreciated? How long has it been since you have heard members of your family expressing appreciation to one another?

The following activities will help your family become more sensitive to each other's good qualities and will provide ways to express appreciation.

A Circle of Appreciation

Start this project at least one day before your family time. Explain that each member of the family is to write a short note of appreciation to each person in the family, expressing why each person is unique, special and appreciated. Suggest that a good way to get ideas to write is to ask yourself: What does (name) mean to me? What are his strong points, his talents, and things I especially like? What do I really appreciate about him?

Each family member should have his appreciation notes completed before family time begins.

As you have your circle of appreciation, appreciate one person at a time. Have each family member read his note to the one being appreciated. Continue until all family members have been appreciated.

Have each family member draw a large circle on an 8½x11-inch sheet of paper (see Fig. 27). Instruct family members to do the following: draw a small circle in the center of the larger circle. Divide the circle into as many sections as there are family members. In the center circle

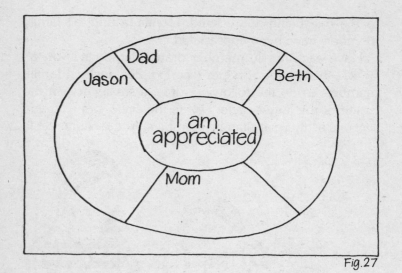

Fig.27

write, "I am appreciated!" In each large section write a name of a family member. Then write what that person appreciates about you (look at "appreciation slips" you used in the circle of appreciation). Repeat this for each section of the circle. Anyone at all surprised of the appreciation?

Help each person feel, "I am really appreciated. I am of value to my family."**

Prayers of Thanksgiving

Gather in a family circle. Join in silent prayer with each person thanking God in his own way. Suggest that each person thank God for other members of the family. Also suggest that each person thank God for His greatness and goodness and His everlasting love.

After your family prayer, read Psalm 100 together and sing favorite songs—your entire family making a "joyful noise" of praise to God.

Bible Readings That Help You Give Thanks

• Ask family members, "What makes *you,* what makes *me,* so special?" Read Genesis 1:26 and Job 33:4 and decide.

• Appoint one member of the family to be the letter writer. Then have everyone in the family suggest one sentence for a prayer-thank-you-letter that thanks God for the good times your family has together. Can you also thank Him for some of the difficult times? What good things happen when the going is rough? See James 1:2-4.

• Read Psalm 8:4-8 to see how important each person is to God. Draw names. Each plan a surprise for the other person to show him how special he is. (Like a note in a lunch bag, or a piece of candy hidden in a shoe!)

• Psalm 136:1 says, "O give thanks unto the Lord; for he is good: for his mercy endureth forever" *(KJV).* List as many of God's qualities as you can. Meditate on each one of these qualities in thanksgiving for the next few minutes.*

• Follow David's command as found in Psalm 147:7. Write a song of thanksgiving or a poem to God right now. It doesn't have to be long or a masterpiece. If you aren't poetic just let what's in your heart flow onto the paper.*

• For your family's devotions read 1 Timothy 6:6-10; Matthew 25:14-30; and Proverbs 31:10-31. List some important material family possessions. Thank God for them, and ask for wisdom in their use.*

* Adapted from *Praying—How to Start and Keep Going,* Bobb Biehl and James W. Hagelganz (Regal Books, 1976). Used by permission.

• Use Psalm 139:14-16 as a guide. Write together a letter of thanks for your family. Everyone contribute!

• Using the buddy system, help one another memorize Acts 17:28 from *The Living Bible*.

• Read Psalm 100:3. Each person pick a favorite word or phrase.

• Take turns reading Psalms 139:14; 100:3, 8:5; 135:1. Thank God together, for so wonderfully making each person.

• For the coming month keep a Thanksgiving chart (see Fig. 28). As a family talk over blessings and problems. Whenever your family honestly can thank God for a situation make a note on the Thanksgiving chart. Use the chart as a guide as you give praise and thanks to God.

Fig. 28

Thanksgiving...

Use this chart to help your family give thanks for specific blessings.

Father, thank You for*

Date	These!

Thank You, Father!

*Jesus, relationships, problems, things, God's work in the lives of others, etc.

Adapted from Praying—How to Start and Keep Going, Bobb Biehl and James W. Hagelganz (Regal Books, 1976). Used by permission.

Celebrate Christmas— It's Jesus Birthday

When That Moment of Wonder Comes

by Frieda Barkman

In my own living room where I weekly vacuum and polish, I have seen the wonder of a little boy kissing the Christ child, and have been startled when a guest heard cathedral chimes from cloud-wreathed towers. Angels have stood outside our window and a deaf child has heard the heavenly choir.

I never know when that moment of wonder will come; but on every anniversary of the good tidings of great joy we get our house ready for the divine appointment. Though we cannot predict how, in His own way, God always appears and the light of His antique glory brings living wonder.

But this Christmas the wonder has not yet come, and it is now New Year's Eve. Flu struck just before Christmas and the family took turns at aches and fever. Relieved to cancel all activities, I leisurely mixed orange juice, took temperatures and dispensed aspirin. I hummed a carol with only a slight twinge of guilt at being so carefree while the others fought the bug.

On Christmas Eve my youngest child John sniffled with teary eyes, "Mom, it doesn't seem like Christmas unless we do the Christmas story." He got the words out bravely.

When my daughter Lisa felt better she too said accusingly, "Mom, it's the one thing we *always* do."

Right. Since she was two years old, we have celebrated "children's night," the night they invite their friends to re-enact the Christmas story. Without it they felt robbed of the wonder.

"Ok," I promised, my heart embracing theirs, "we'll do it after Christmas, as soon as everyone is well."

So, when family fevers finally abated, everyone went to work to put the wonder back into Christmas. Invitations were made by telephone. Folks were less busy after Christmas and glad to come. The redwood manger was filled with shreds of brown paper bags (straw is hard to come by in the city unless you own a horse). Lisa scrubbed and wrapped Baby Dear in swaddling clothes made from

an old white sheet. I pressed and sorted the costumes, putting them in various rooms to avoid confusion.

And now on New Year's Eve we stand in a circle and my husband Paul prays, "We invite You too, Lord Jesus. Come, be born under our roof today."

As we stand and wait for our guests we recall past wonders.

John, who does not know a Christmas without this ritual, remembers our youngest and shyest guest last year.

"Matti wouldn't be a wise man and he wouldn't be a shepherd either, but when it was all over he ran to the manger where Baby Dear lay wrapped in swaddling clothes and hugged and kissed it."

Those of us who watched knew that Matti understood. The Christ child was real and Matti had kissed the doll in the simple faith and wonder of childhood. His wonder became our wonder.

Wonder comes in different ways. Maybe when the angels sing. Angels? People don't believe in angels anymore. And if they did appear most people would look for the ropes and pulleys. But children sometimes hear angels at Christmas.

My husband Paul smiles as he remembers the children's first encounter with a heavenly visit. It was a cold December night when, sitting at the dinner table, our starry-eyed twosome suddenly cried, "Listen!" College students, knee-deep in snow, stood outside our window and sang Christmas into our wondering ears. Paul questioned whether we had shattered the children's faith by turning on the lights and illuminating the carolers.

He need not have wondered long. Lisa, six then, caught the angels' song. After dinner, with all the knowledge of a few piano lessons, she found the carol on the keys. She practiced diligently, with only one finger, making joyous

Christmas music. That hushed Advent night she confided, "Mommie, 'Silent Night' sounds like a prayer. I think I'll pray it on my knees." And she did. And together in our hearts we heard the angels sing.

Recalling all these flashes of wonder, Paul concluded, "God always keeps His appointments, regardless of our stuffy traditions of time and place. What should keep Him from salvaging the wonder for us on New Year's Eve?"

Here are the neighbors now! Our little guests, with parents in tow, walk up the lighted path. The white plumber's candles in coffee jars framing the walk flicker as if to announce that the transformation has begun. Sheets and tinsel ropes change girls into angels; bathrobes, staves and towels produce authentic shepherds; a woolly lamb stuffed with courage bolsters the littlest shepherd.

Suddenly panic comes from Father's study: "We're short a wise man!" So we draft a parent from our living-room theater-in-the-round to stand in. Next there's a cry for more safety pins from the angel department and a complaint that the halos itch. Otherwise all is in readiness.

It happens simply, naturally, unrehearsed. When my husband Paul reads the warm, beloved words of St. Luke, "And it came to pass in those days..." our living room becomes a hillside in Bethlehem. Shepherds decked in towels emerge from the bathroom; angels in white descend the stairs with arms outstretched. Standing on tiptoe, these hovering angels almost leave earth even as the heavenly host almost touched it. Wise men pace through the hall marked, "Detour to Jerusalem." All find their way to kneel at the manger, where a serene, blue-draped Mary sits guarded by her brave Joseph.

Then everyone in that room joins to sing reverently, "Away in a Manger" and "Silent Night." We close with a simple prayer of thanks for the Babe who came to be our

Saviour and whose birthday we honor. Sometimes even parents slip silently to their knees.

Adults who have lost the glow find it again, for this is the night we are all children and see with other eyes. A photographer sent by the local newspaper stays to worship. Our wise men in rich ebony, our angels in oriental grace (our neighbors are international) remind us that Christmas is for all people. It is when we share Christmas with others that the moment of wonder is most likely to happen.

Still in their costumes, the children find pillows and rugs and settle around the tree. It is time to read the story that may open the door for some. But what about our little deaf neighbor, Andrew?

Out of the corner of my eye I watch him as I read. At first his face is empty. His eyes wander around the room—to the angels on the tree, to the many glowing candles. But wait—I don't know what private visitation is taking place in his silent world—it is there, the radiance and the wonder! He too has *done* Christmas. It has come again.

But the moment of hushed reverence never lasts long. Soon shepherds, wise men and angels return to the bedrooms and re-emerge normal, exuberant and often noisy boys and girls. As parents resume everyday conversation I bring out the punch and goodies. Invariably some child whispers to me, "I hope we can come again next year."

They will come again and we will stand on the threshold of a new miracle. Could that be the mysterious intrigue of Christmas—that its wonder has appeared anew for each of two thousand years, and will continue to appear in all the years to come?

What is the wonder? It is Jesus Himself come to visit under our roof and in our hearts. No lesser guest will do.

—Adapted from *Look for the Wonder* (Regal Books, 1975).

How to Help Young Children Discover the Real Christmas

by Margaret Self

Christmas! The word itself brings feelings of extraordinary excitement. And rightly so. Even a young child is stirred by the wonder of wonders. But let's be sure he knows what the excitement is really about.

How can parents handle the task of helping young children realize that Christmas is a celebration of gratitude to God for His unspeakable gift of love? Here are suggestions for ways you can make the biblical and spiritual aspects of Christmas meaningful and attractive to your youngsters.

Help your child know the simple facts of Jesus' birth as they are recorded in Scripture.

• Read the story of the first Christmas to your child from Bible storybooks as well as from an easy-to-understand version of the Bible.

• Visit your Christian bookstore and choose books that will appeal to your child. Both *The Bible Story Picture Book* and *It Didn't Just Happen* (Regal Books) include the Christmas story along with discussion questions and comments.

• Buy an unbreakable nativity scene set and let your children use the figures to "play out" the Christmas story.

Help your child feel that Jesus is God's best gift of love to him.

• Remember, much of a child's response is a reflection of the attitudes he lives with.

• Nurture feelings of joy, love and thankfulness in your child with your own good feelings.

• Avoid the hurry and busyness of Christmas that makes young children feel alone...left out.

• Talk about giving thanks to God for Jesus in the presence of your children.

• Include children in family plans for expressing love for Jesus by caring and loving others. (Make cookies for elderly relatives, shut-ins, etc. Send cards to friends. Plan surprises for grandparents, etc.)

Help your child express his joy, excitement and feelings of love.

• Include children in making Christmas decorations, gifts and cards for members of the family and friends.

• Help your child feel gladness as you sing the songs of Christmas.

• Be sensitive to moments when it is natural to talk about God and to encourage your child to talk to God with thanks and praise.

Keep Santa in the proper perspective.

• Avoid referring to Santa as a real person.

• Avoid the "What do you want Santa to bring you for Christmas?" and "Be good for Santa" emphasis.

• When your child wants to talk about Santa Claus, listen attentively. Then say, "That's fun. Santa's a happy pretend fellow."

• Keep the meaning of Christmas clear by frequently commenting, "Christmas is a happy time because it is Jesus' birthday."

• Bake a birthday cake for Jesus. Children especially understand that because Christmas is Jesus' birthday there should be a cake! Sing "Happy Birthday" to Jesus and plan together what your family can give Him for a gift of love.

Remember and Retell the Christmas Story

Your children will enjoy remembering and talking about the Christmas story when you involve them in these activities.

Nativity 'Dinner Guests'

Place a different figure of the nativity scene in front of each family member's plate at dinner. Ask each person to share what that character of the Christmas story gave because he loved. (Ideas: Joseph gave Jesus a home. Shepherds gave time to go see Jesus, gave praise to God...etc.) Encourage each person to think of what he can give because he loves Jesus.

A Christmas Poem

Your young child will enjoy learning the poem "Mary's Secret" and saying it with you. The simple motions help you share facts of the Christmas story.

Mary's Secret Luke 1:26-31,34,35

Mary was praying,
a bright angel came.
"You'll soon have a baby,
Lord Jesus His name."

"And who is His father?"
"The Lord God above.
He's sending dear Jesus
to show His great love."
Oh, wonderful secret!
The good news was true.

For God sent dear Jesus
to love me and you!

—Judith B. Kaiser

Finger Puppet Christmas Play

Let your fingers tell the Christmas story.

Materials: Paper, crayons, paints or marking pens, scissors, glue.

Procedure: Each person draws and colors the head of one or more characters from the Christmas story (Baby Jesus, Mary, Joseph, Magi, Innkeeper, etc.). Attach the heads to paper strips which are glued to fit around the fingers. (See Fig. 29.)

Re-enact the Christmas story with each person taking

one or more parts. This can be very simple or more complicated, depending upon your children's ages.

Use: To review the Christmas story, and to teach its meaning in a creative manner. Use Luke 2:8-20 and Matthew 2:1-12 for your study and script guide.

Fig. 29

Christmas Story Hanging

Help your youngster create a vertical Christmas story hanging (see Fig. 30) to help him get acquainted with the story of the first Christmas.

Cut Christmas story pictures from old Christmas cards: manger scene, angels, shepherds, wise men, etc. Mount pictures on construction paper and link together with yarn tied through punched holes.

Make this project more meaningful by talking about the Christmas story as you work together.

Or, make Christmas pictures. Glue or tape Christmas card scenes to 9x12-inch pieces of construction paper. To make pictures more meaningful, add lettering such as "Angels told the shepherds about baby Jesus," or "God loved us and sent the Lord Jesus," etc.

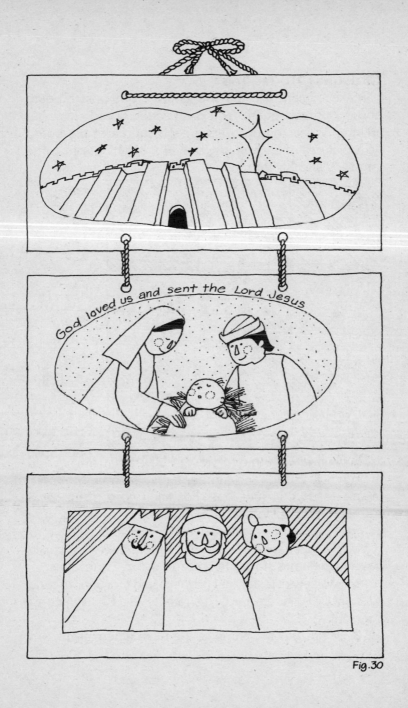

Fig. 30

Christmas Tic-Tac-Toe

Make a giant Tic-Tac-Toe board from poster board about 2x2-feet square. You can use the board plain, but children will enjoy decorating each square of the board with pictures of Christmas. (See Fig. 31).) Cut out some large O's and X's for markers.

Fig. 31

Divide the family into two teams. Give one team O's and the other X's. Dad—or another family member not on a team—reads the questions. For each correct answer a team member places one marker on the Tic-Tac-Toe board. The first team with three in a row wins.

You will need a list of about 20 simple questions based on the Christmas story. Here are 10 sample questions:

1. What Old Testament prophet said that Jesus would be called "Wonderful," "The Mighty God," "Prince of Peace"?

2. What was the name of the town where Jesus was born?

3. What New Testament prophet helped people know why Jesus came to earth?

4. Who was the king of Judea when Jesus was born?

5. What town in Galilee was home for Joseph and Mary?

6. Who told the shepherds that Jesus was born?

7. True or False. King Herod was happy to hear Jesus was born.

8. What gifts did the wise men bring to Jesus?

9. True or False. Only three angels said, "Glory to God in the highest..."

10. How did they dress the newborn baby Jesus?

Prophets Who Told of Jesus' Coming

Hundreds of years before Christ was born, God chose special messengers called prophets to tell the Good News: God would send *His Son, the Saviour, into the world.*

Following (in code) is a message about Jesus that the prophet Isaiah gave to the people of his time. Work together to decode Isaiah's words. Code:

A B C D E F G H I J K L M N O P Q R S T
0 2 ½ ¢ ? _ 5 % * 7 # $ () @ 8 + = 3 9 4
U V W X Y Z
! 1 6 .. / ¼

       _ 8 3   ! @ 4 8   ! 9   0

Message: _ _ _ _ _ _ _ _ _

½ % * $ ¢   * 9 2 8 3 @ ! @ 4 8 ! 9

_ _ _ _ _ _ _ _ _ _ _ _ _ _ _ _ _

0 9 8 @ * 9 5 * 1 ? @

_ _ _ _ _ _ _ _ _ _ _   (Isaiah 9:6)

'Twas the Week Before Christmas... with Kids in the House

by Mary Louise Kitsen

Outside it's cold and wintry. Inside it's unhappy and noisy. It's the week before Christmas and all the kids are in the house clamoring, "What can we do now?"

Trouble is, the children have waited too long for Christmas. They are frustrated and impatient. They have seen Christmas in the stores...on TV...and poured over the pictures of toys in the newspapers. When will it ever come?

Not only is this a difficult time for children and parents, it's a time when the true spirit and meaning of Christmas can get lost unless you have good plans for keeping everyone busy that week before Christmas.

Here are simple ways you can be prepared to make those days happier ones.

Gift Wrapping Fun

Save a few special gifts for the children to wrap. Especially set aside the gifts for grandparents and encourage the children to help each other do the wrapping. Don't worry if the packages aren't wrapped to perfection. Just think of Grandma and Grandpa's face when the children say, "We wrapped that gift."

I-Love-You Christmas Cards

Get together a box of Christmas card makings: construction paper, small pieces of Christmas gift-wrapping paper, crayons, felt pens and Christmas stickers. Then early in the week before Christmas let the children make their own I-Love-You Christmas cards for special people in their lives. Maybe a teacher, a favorite babysitter, a neighbor, a playmate or relatives...grandparents, aunts, uncles and cousins. If the greeting must travel many miles, send it air mail. Or if the destination is in your own town, have fun on a Christmas-card-delivery excursion.

Celebrate with a Treat

While you are out mailing and delivering the cards stop to have a treat, perhaps some hot chocolate. And while you're enjoying the treat, talk about the reasons for sending Christmas cards. Share ideas on how you feel when you get a Christmas card—especially one with a personal note. Time consuming? Sure it is. But you'll really feel the Christmas spirit as you celebrate by enjoying time with your children.

Cookies to Share

Bake cookies—with everyone helping—for the children to share with their friends. You'll be too busy the week before Christmas? Probably. That is...unless you've gotten shopping and other chores out of the way earlier in December to make time to enjoy the week before Christmas with your children.

Christmas Story Place Mats

When the children become restless, read to them about

that first Christmas in Bethlehem. Then bring out a box of old Christmas cards with pictures of the Christmas story: angels, shepherds, wise men, etc. Supply each child with a place mat-size piece of shelf paper, scissors (blunt nose if the children are young) and paste. Encourage each child to create his own Christmas story scenes on his place mat from the pictures he's cut from the cards. Let any of the children who wish make two place mats, so there will be one for Mother and Dad and any guest who may drop by. The blessing in this project is that you bring the Christmas story into focus and help the children to think about it for awhile—all without preaching.

Christmas Preview

A couple or three evenings before Christmas have a preview of the holiday. After the evening meal, gather the family around. Discuss the reason for giving gifts at Christmas. Talk about God's love and His "unspeakable" gift. Say 2 Corinthians 9:15 together as a prayer. Then give each child one small pre-Christmas gift brightly wrapped. A Christmas story coloring book and new box of crayons for each child is a good gift. Take time to choose gifts each child will enjoy and in some way help him/her keep the true meaning of Christmas in focus.

Dad and Mother Together

Planning for good ways to use the week before Christmas shouldn't be "Mom's problem." Instead make it a "Mom and Dad" project. Together you can come up with all kinds of ideas that can make the week a special time for your family. Let other things go undone and share Christmas week with your youngsters. You'll find it well worth the effort. And you'll discover a special joy in Christmas for you and your children.

Creative Christmas Collection

By Sandy Rau and Pat Holt

Philippians 4:4 tells us to "Always be full of joy in the Lord; I say it again, REJOICE!"—even amidst the hurry of the busy Christmas season! Take time to rejoice and to spend happy hours making things as a family.

Pick a Star

Materials: Toothpicks, aluminum foil, glitter (silver is best), glue, white thread.

Procedure: Roll a piece of aluminum foil into a tight ball until it is about the size of a golf ball. Working over a sheet of newspaper, dip toothpicks into glue and roll in glitter. Lay on paper to dry. When dry, insert the toothpicks into the foil ball to form a star. (See Fig. 32.) Attach the thread. Your star is ready for the Christmas tree.

Note: if you are working with very young children, have them watch while you do the "glitter step" for them.

Use: Christmas tree ornament or a mobile.

Fig. 32

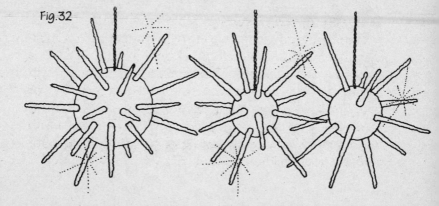

Patchwork Bells

Materials: White construction paper, scissors, glue, scraps of Christmas wrapping paper.

Procedure: Precut the bell shapes out of construction paper or let the children cut the bells you have outlined on the paper. Cut and paste small pieces of the bright Christmas wrap onto the bell. Decorate both sides. Make a hole at the top of the bell. Attach a bit of red or green yarn and it is ready for your Christmas tree. The bells are such fun, each child may want to make two or three. (See Fig. 33.)

Use: Christmas ornaments or gift tags. Or even a Christmas card that will hang from a friend's tree.

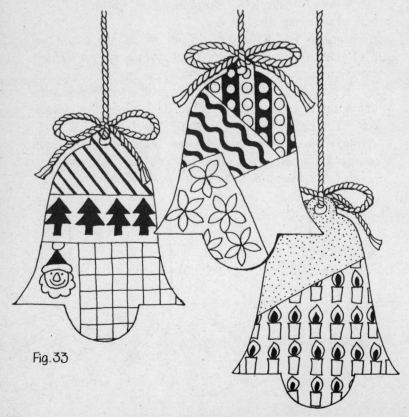

Fig. 33

Golden Snowflake Tree

Materials: Fifteen white, gold or silver doilies (6-8 inches in diameter); masking tape.

Procedure: Choose a large wall area or the back of a door to decorate. Arrange doilies on the floor or a large table in a Christmas tree pattern (see Fig. 34). Bottom row, 5 doilies; next row, 4 doilies; next row, 3 doilies; next row, 2 doilies; finish, 1 doily, top of the tree! Roll masking tape pieces into a circle and place on the back of each doily. Stick doilies to wall or door in the pattern explained above. (Do not use double-stick tape for this as it might remove paint when taken down.)

Use: Decoration—pretty as is. You may want to cut out interesting and significant pictures from old Christmas cards to place in the center of each doily. Or, even hang a special Christmas card in the center of each doily as a way to display your favorites.

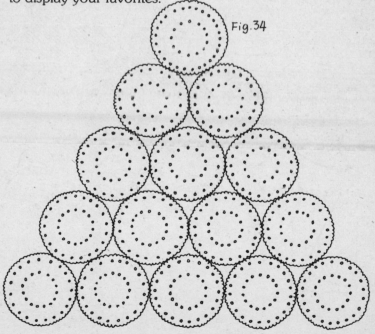

Fig. 34

Angel Decorations or Cards

Cut strings of angel figures from shelf paper or shiny gift-wrap paper. (See Fig. 35.) Cut strings of four or five angels at a time. Then glue them together to make a chain long enough to reach around the tree.

Strings of angel figures also make attractive Christmas cards. For each card let your child glue two strings of figures together so you have eight angels. Letter "Glory to God and on earth, peace" with one word on each of seven angels. Glue a photo of your child's face on the last angel figure and help him letter his name. (See Fig. 35.) You may want to make this a special card for close relatives.

Fig. 35

A Christmas Box for Jesus

Make a "Christmas Box for Jesus" to open on Christmas Day (see Fig. 36). Encourage each person in the family to make a Christmas card for Jesus and place it in the box. On each card write, "Dear Jesus, I will give my love this Christmas by doing the following: _____

_____
_____ "

In his note each person describes the kind of Christmas project he will do for someone in the name of Jesus *before* Christmas. Here are a few suggestions:

Cheer up a friend who is lonely and unhappy.... Tell grandparents that you love them. Maybe write them a note or letter, or make a surprise phone call.... Make cookies to share with neighbors.... Surprise someone in the family by offering to help with a task.... Write a note or letter to a missionary.... Think up your own "giving to Jesus" ideas.

Place the cards in the box for Jesus and put it under the tree. On Christmas Day open the box, read the cards, and have each person tell how his "gift for Jesus" worked out. If someone didn't get to put his gift idea into action encourage him/her to go ahead—even after Christmas.

Fig. 36

Tabletop "Praise Tree"

Obtain a small table-size Christmas tree to decorate with notes of praise and thanksgiving to God for the blessings of the year. Near the tree have a tray of cards (prepared with red and green yarn for tying). Provide pen or pencils and encourage family members and friends to write their thoughts of praise, on the cards. Tie each card to the tree as a gift of thanksgiving to the heavenly Father (see Fig. 37).

Fig. 37

Tradition Can Sneak Up on You

by Phyllis Reynolds Naylor

I can remember how often I've looked wistfully at old-fashioned scenes on Christmas cards and wished that our family had some holiday traditions.

Why couldn't we go into the forest looking for yule logs, I wondered. Why couldn't we bundle up in red and green scarves and go caroling? Why couldn't we have candle-light processions up and down the staircase, or roast pig with an apple in its mouth, and a Christmas pageant played out before admiring relatives? Tradition, that's what I want—big healthy chunks of it to remember when I'm old and gray.

As I was baking my usual Swedish almond cookies the other night, however, I heard the children talking in the next room.

"This is the part of Christmas I like best," Susan was saying, "when Mom makes all the cookies and the house smells good for days. She always does the almond cookies first, then the chocolate curls, and then the lemon bars."

Do I? I wondered. You mean there's a pattern to my holiday baking that the children detected and enjoyed?

"I like mailing the packages," Peter commented. "And putting on the seals."

Mailing packages? I choked. That was a tradition? Well, sort of. Since our relatives are scattered all over the continental United States, there comes a week early in December when the gifts are wrapped, packed in boxes, decorated with seals, and carted off in the back of the station wagon to the post office.

"You've got to be kidding," said Jack. "Nothing is better than Christmas Eve."

"Yeah," said Susan, "we always build a fire, and sit around looking at the old picture albums."

"And Mom puts a plate of fudge on the table," added Peter.

And we turn out all the lights except those on the Christmas tree and look at the shadows," said Jack.

"And call Gramps," said Peter.

"And walk to the midnight service at church. Remember the year it was snowing and Dad pulled us there on the sled?" Susan remembered.

Glory be, we do have traditions! I thought. We're creating them each time we repeat something that's fun and meaningful to the whole family. Never mind that it's a pilgrimage to the post office instead of the forest; never mind that fudge takes the place of wassail (whatever that is) or that photo albums entertain us in place of a candlelight procession.

Tradition creeps up on us when we least suspect it, and I rather imagine I'll have lots to remember when I'm old and gray.

Send a Freezer to Jesus...?

Have you ever wishfully wondered what it would be like to break out of the annual "Christmas gift exchange" tradition and do something more meaningful with the money?

Wayne and Terry Pearson of Thousand Oaks, California tried it, and it worked out beautifully, despite some awkward moments with parents and in-laws.

It all started when they began talking about how they wished Christmas included more than remembering relatives with gifts they didn't really need. The more Wayne and Terry talked about it the more certain they became that celebrating Jesus' birthday should mean gifts for Jesus. At last they decided what they would do.

First came the letters to the relatives...

Dear Mom & Dad,

This is a Merry Christmas and a Happy Birthday letter.
You know how much we enjoy remembering both of
you—and the other relatives too—when birthdays come.
Just thinking about this helped us to decide how we want
to celebrate Christmas this year—by remembering Jesus
on His birthday.

That's why we're writing, to explain that instead of
buying Christmas gifts for everyone in the family this year,
we're buying a freezer for Dan and Karen, a couple we
know who have a home up in the San Gabriel canyon.
They have a real mission sharing the gospel with young
people who've written off the establishment and are trying
to find their way in a new life-style. Some are hippies, some
are runaways and strays—all with many questions and
problems and usually hungry. The freezer will be a big help
to Dan and Karen because with the small refrigerator they
have, it is almost impossible for them to buy a supply of
food that lasts more than a couple of days with all of the
mouths they feed.

And one more thing—instead of the gifts you usually
send our way, we'd like for you to take that money and buy
something for someone who has a real need. Please give it
as a gift for Jesus.

We send our love and best wishes for a merry and
blessed Christmas, and as you know, we're hoping your
Christmas plans will include some days here with us.
With love,

Wayne & Jerry

Giving the freezer turned out to be an adventure in many ways...

Wayne's parents did come to visit for the holidays, but not in the usual way bringing gifts. In fact, there seemed to be a few uneasy feelings about the new plans for celebrating Christmas as Jesus' birthday without the usual exchange of gifts.

But an unexpected blessing was in store. On the day the freezer was to be delivered there was a phone call from the delivery men. Sure they had taken the freezer up into the canyon, but no way would they carry it up the 150 steep steps to the house.

Wayne enlisted the help of his father. When they arrived in the canyon, Dan joined them to accomplish the task of inching the freezer up and up the difficult stairs. The blessing came with the fellowship and feeling of joy that transpired between Wayne's somewhat skeptical father and Dan, a vibrant young Christian with a deep, sincere sense of enjoyment in serving Jesus.

As Wayne recalls that day, he says, "Together we all experienced thankfulness for each other and for the freezer—truly a gift for Jesus."

Banner Birthday Party for Jesus

Making family Christmas banners was the highlight of a Jesus Birthday Celebration at Bob and Margie Hammer's home in Delanco, New Jersey.

The idea started to take shape when Margie asked the five young mothers who meet with her for Bible study and coffee each Wednesday morning how they would feel about getting their families together for a "Jesus birthday celebration" on a Sunday afternoon before Christmas. Everyone liked the idea and planning got under way. They decided that the celebration would include each family making a Christmas banner, sharing the Christmas story, visiting together over simple refreshments and a time of singing carols with Margie accompanying on the guitar.

One girl purchased the basic banner materials: heavy green cloth and gold braid, along with the dowel rods and yarn for hanging the banners. Each girl took banner makings home to do some preliminary preparation, like hemming the top for the dowel rod, sewing on gold braid across

the top, and such. More important, each family started to think of how they would make their banner. What would it say? How would it look?

Margie recalls, "For banner ideas we really tried to tune in on what the different ones in the family were thinking about Christmas. For example, if a child said something about Christmas being Jesus' birthday we talked about that as a possible theme for our banner."

When the special Sunday afternoon finally came and everyone arrived at the Hammers', the group included the six couples and their children: three boys—two, three and seven; and three girls—a three- and a four-year-old and an eight-month-old baby who happily watched the activities in the downstairs family room from her bouncing doorway swing. There was also the grandmother visiting the Hammers who played an important role appreciating the children, helping with refreshments and thoroughly enjoying all the activities.

As Margie remembers that afternoon, she says, "The fun thing was that each family was really involved in making its Christmas banner. No matter how small the children were they did something. Some helped cut shapes and letters and decorations. Everyone wanted to share and see the other banners. The banners were all great. One family had cut out felt letters before they came that said, 'Christmas Is Jesus' Birthday' and glued them to their banner with a picture of the manger scene and a birthday cake.

"Another family used glue and thick yarn to write in raised bright handwriting: 'Thank You for This Gift.'

"One banner had a manger scene with the legs of the manger made of twigs from a tree in the family's yard. The manger on another banner was made of Popsicle sticks with the baby lying on hay—a bit of yellow Easter-basket kind of grass. Each banner was definitely the only one of its kind in the whole world!"

After the banners were finished everyone went upstairs and gathered around the large manger scene that is a family treasure at the Hammer house (made by Margie's father years ago). As one of the mothers read the Christmas story from a book written especially for young children, each youngster took his turn placing a character of the Christmas story on the straw-covered stable floor.

"A surprising quietness filled the room as we shared in a prayer of thanksgiving to Jesus for His love. And after the prayer we all felt close to each other as we visited together sharing cake, cookies, punch and ice cream. Soon the children settled down with their families as we all enjoyed singing the carols together.

"As everyone left with their banners, inviting each other to stop by and see how the banners looked actually 'hung,' we felt good—like we had really celebrated Jesus' birthday and been close to Him."

Celebrate!
Jesus Is Born

Advent Is a Joyful Time

Advent is a time of joy for all Christians because it is the season when we prepare for the celebration of Christ's birth. Advent begins on the fourth Sunday before Christmas and ends on Christmas Eve. For many years Christians all over the world have used an Advent wreath made with candles and Christmas greens as a worship center for family devotional times during the weeks before Christmas.

These family time activities will help your family celebrate a blessed time of Advent and enjoy the true meaning of Christmas: the birth of our Lord and Saviour, Jesus Christ.

Make an Advent Wreath

To make an Advent wreath you will need: a styrofoam base, 12 inches in diameter, and at least 1 inch thick; 5 candles—4 red, 8 inches high; 1 white, 10 inches high; plastic Christmas greens and any other desired ornaments such as pine cones.

Use a table knife to cut five triangular holes in the styrofoam base for the candles. (Make each hole a bit smaller than the base of the candle.) The white candle goes in the center, the red candles are evenly spaced around the outside edge (see Fig. 38).

Wrap the base of each candle with a bit of floral clay and push straight down into hole. (Don't wiggle it around or you'll make the hole too big and the candle will be loose.)

Use pins to fasten the plastic greenery to the styrofoam base and pine cones for decoration. (Note: You can use real evergreen branches, but they will dry out in a short time and become a fire hazard. Regardless of what you use, always be sure a parent is present when the wreath is lighted.)

When the wreath is made, do not pick it up by the candles, because they can become loose or crooked. (If a candle happens to loosen, cut a new hole and reinsert it in the styrofoam.)

Lighting the Advent Candles

These devotional thoughts will help you plan Bible readings and comments to share with your family each week during Advent as you light the candles of the Advent wreath.

WEEK 1. Light one red candle of the Advent wreath. As it burns explain that hundreds of years before Jesus was born, special men called prophets wrote that Jesus would someday come to be the Saviour of the world. One of

Fig. 38

these prophets was Isaiah and he wrote this: (read Isaiah 7:14).

Close your first Advent worship time in prayer. *Don't hurry things,* but reverently talk about how God promised to send Jesus to be our Saviour and how glad we are to remember Jesus' birthday each year at Christmas. Suggest that each family member thank God for another Christmas season and for what Christmas really means because of Jesus Christ.

WEEK 2. Light two red candles of the Advent wreath, then turn to Luke 1:26-38 in *The Living Bible.*

If possible, let several family members share in reading. If a younger child wants to read, allow him to read a verse or two, but be careful older children don't get bored by letting it drag.

After reading, comment: "This story tells us how God prepared Mary for the birth of Jesus. He told her what would happen, how she had been chosen for a very, very special purpose—to be the mother of Jesus. Let's stop and talk right now about how we can prepare for Jesus' birthday."

Before having prayer, discuss:

1. How can our entire family prepare for Christmas? What can we do to remind us that Jesus' birthday is what Christmas is all about?

2. How can our family prepare others for Christmas? What can we give or do that helps us reach out to others in Jesus' name?

Pray together and talk to the Lord about what you think He wants you and your family to do this Christmastime. Don't rush through prayer, or make it mechanical. Some families find it very meaningful to hold hands as they pray.

WEEK 3. Light three red candles of the Advent wreath. As they burn read John 3:16. Talk together about why this can be called a Christmas Bible verse. Then read 2 Corinthians 9:15 aloud and repeat it together until you can all say it from memory. Talk together about why Jesus is such a wonderful gift to all people. Compare 2 Corinthians 9:15 with John 3:16. How are the verses alike?

Pray together and thank God for eternal life through belief in Jesus Christ. Repeat the words of 2 Corinthians 9:15 together as part of your prayer.

Creative members of your family will enjoy trying to put down on paper why Jesus is so wonderful. Let the family poets do their thing; others may want to write a brief letter to Jesus and thank Him for all He has done in their lives.

WEEK 4. Light the four red candles of the Advent wreath. Read Psalm 95:1,2. Do what the Psalm says and sing your favorite Christmas carols. Praise God together. Now that it is almost Christmastime everyone is busy thinking about getting things ready for Christmas Day! Gifts are on everyone's mind. So read again about God's gift in 2 Corinthians 9:15 and compare with Romans 6:23.

What can each person have for his own gift from God because Jesus came?

Pray together giving thanks, and then before you sing "O Come All Ye Faithful" have a child read Psalm 95:1,2. Let your song be a "psalm of praise."

IT'S CHRISTMAS EVE! Light all of the candles of the Advent wreath. As the candles shine gather round while Dad or some member of the family reads or tells the Christmas story from Luke 2:1-20. Encourage everyone to imagine they are on the hillside with the shepherds... imagine you can hear the angels sing and see their brightness in the sky... think how it must have been to go to Bethlehem and see the Baby Jesus.

Pray together and thank God for His gift of love, the Lord Jesus Christ. As the candles burn bright, read Jesus' words from John 8:12 and sing "Joy to the World." Jesus' birthday is a happy time!

An Alternate Idea for Christmas Eve

After the candles of the Advent wreath are lighted, bring forward a beautifully wrapped gift addressed to your family. Have a family member repeat 2 Corinthians 9:15 and then comment: About now everyone is thinking of gifts he's going to get and gifts he's going to give. If you stop to think about it, there are two sides to a gift: giving and receiving. You need both, if it's to be a gift. No matter what it costs, or how nice it's wrapped, it won't be a real gift until it's accepted and opened. You can't force a gift on anyone; you can only offer it."

Open the package, which should contain an entire Bible and mark at Luke 2:1-20. Let different family members share in reading the passage. Then repeat John 3:16 together aloud and pray together for people who have not yet received God's "indescribable gift."

Christmas Isn't Over

Make *un*-decorating an important time of remembering the true and lasting meanings of Christmas.

Christmas Lights

As your family packs away the Christmas candles and takes the lights off the Christmas tree, remind your children that sometimes Christmas is called "Festival of Lights." Get ideas from the family about how the lights of Christmas can remind us of Jesus.

Have one of the older children read John 8:12. Talk

together about what it means when we say *Jesus is the light of the world.* (For ideas read Ps. 27:1; 2 Cor. 4:6; John 14:6.)

The Christmas Tree

As you un-decorate the Christmas tree talk about some of the ways the Christmas tree is a reminder of important truths about Jesus. For example, the evergreen tree is a reminder of God's everlasting love and the everlasting life Jesus came to give. Emphasize this by telling an old German Christmas tree legend. The story goes...

One Christmas Eve, Boniface—a Christian missionary who carried the gospel into Europe in the early 700's—found people worshiping an oak tree. Boniface told them they should worship God, not a tree, and he took his axe and chopped down the oak.

Nearby stood a small evergreen tree. "Look," said Boniface, "here is a tree that reminds us of God. Its needles are always green reminding us of God's everlasting love and the everlasting life He gives. At the top of the tree is a single branch, like a finger, always pointing us to God."

(This may or may not be the origin of the use of the Christmas tree. But the words attributed to Boniface do give the Christmas tree new and meaningful significance.)

Down... but Not Forgotten

As you take down the Christmas decorations and pack them away, talk about ways that Christmas isn't over. Ask: What are things about Christmas that can't be packed away? For ideas read John 3:16; Romans 6:23; Ephesians 2:8.

Use 2 Corinthians 9:15 as a prayer of thanks for the wonderful gift of Jesus and the truths of Christmas that can never be packed away. They are forever.

Sharing Your Christmas Tree

Little children will enjoy a backyard Christmas tree to share with the birds. After the tree has been un-decorated, take tree outside and redecorate with bread crusts, suet, lettuce and bits of apple. You can sprinkle birdseed on the branches and under the tree.

The special fun is watching quietly from a window as the birds have their Christmas party.

As you watch, talk with your children about all of the wonderful things God gives to us: each other to enjoy... the birds... all outdoors... and most of all His love, and Jesus, our friend and Saviour.

Happy New Year— Family Style

It was New Year's Eve, and my wife and I were headed for our usual "watchnight" events at church—but Kim, Jeff and Todd, ages 14, 12 and 10 at the time, were not taking this one in stride.

"How come we can't go out on New Year's?"

"You never spend New Year's with us."

"Why can't we have a party and stuff?"

"Yes, er...we'll have to talk about this...see you next year, gang." And off we fled to spend a rather guilt-ridden evening. That night we both resolved to spend the next New Year's Eve as a total family.

As the following New Year's Eve approached, we all started wondering if it wouldn't be fun to invite one or two other families to join our party. It turned out that three other families we knew had gotten the same idea on their own. Most of their children matched ours in age. The wives conferred briefly on the phone, and in no time at all our "family cluster" New Year's Eve party was "Go!"

Our format was simple: plenty of good food (potluck style), lots of fun with crazy games, and some fellowship with the Lord to help us all commit the new year to Him.

We opened with the food—topped by the gastronomic hit of the evening (at least in the opinion of the kids present)—chocolate fondue.

Then came games: an indoor scavenger hunt... a wild, shoes-off relay (passing a volleyball using feet only) ... "thread the spoon" (a fascinating exercise in which you run a spoon with yarn tied to it through your clothes from collar to cuff and then pass the spoon on to the next person).

Next came a time of sharing that inspired a thoughtful look back at the year that was gone. We took turns remembering...

The best thing about our vacation:

The worst thing about our vacation:

My biggest goof last year:

Our biggest crises:

The most fun we had as a family:

The most interesting person I met:

The biggest problem I faced:

Jesus helped me most when:

The discussion was really flowing now, so we shifted to priorities for the new year:

Next year our family should...

Do more...

Be more...

Go more often to...

Then, pre-cut paper leaves (a contribution from our daughter Kim) were passed out and each person wrote down one bad habit he or she wanted to break. Symbolically, we tossed our leaves into the glowing fireplace. More paper leaves were distributed as we each wrote down our resolutions for the new year. I don't recall too many of the "new leaf vows," but I do remember that several of the children resolved to "spend more fun times together like tonight." *That* was worth the whole thing, and it also fit in perfectly with our verse for the evening—Romans 5:2 in *The Living Bible* paraphrase:

"For because of our faith, he has brought us into this place of highest privilege where we now stand, and we confidently and joyfully look forward to actually becoming all that God has had in mind for us to be."

We closed our devotional time by joining hands in one big circle and praying together. (Again, more requests for time together as families.)

From there to midnight it was more food, more fun, more crazy games. Relay teams competed in "sweat suit balloon stuff" (seeing how many balloons they could blow up and stuff inside an oversized sweat suit worn by a smaller team member). Then we all struggled with "Twister," a commercial game seemingly designed to dismember (or at least disjoint) players over 30.

Midnight approached and there was a mad scramble for noisemakers—pots, pans—anything to make a racket. I wound up, somehow, with a hub cap and jack handle from the trunk of my car. We all poured into the street in front of the house. Jeff, my 13-year-old, readied a skyrocket he had produced from somewhere in the maze of his room.

Twelve o'clock struck—and so did we—banging and cheering wildly the arrival of the new year. Jeff's skyrocket went off beautifully and soared heavenward as if to say, "Make this year the best one yet!!"

As I beat contentedly on my hub cap, I distinctly recall thinking: "This is the best New Year's celebration I've ever had!"

And later, as we wound down our family fling, just about everybody at the party said the same.

Our families have gotten together for other parties since then, and they've been great, but there's something I'll never forget about our first "Family New Year's Eve Party."

Thanks, Lord... thanks for the memory...

Plan Your New Year's Eve Party

If you want to try the games the Ridenours used at their party, here are basic directions:

Indoor Scavenger Hunt

Divide into teams and choose 10-15 items that people can find easily on their person or in the room. First team to get all items to the judge wins.

Thread the Spoon

Divide into two teams. For each team, cut a long piece of yarn (20 feet or more) and tie one end to a spoon. At the signal, each team has to "thread the spoon" through the clothes worn by team members. First person begins at the top and works the spoon to the bottom. Next person takes spoon and works from bottom to top, and so it goes to the end of the line, making sure not to break the yarn (which "ties" everyone together). First team finished wins. Note: it's best to alert all the ladies coming to the party to wear casual clothes—pantsuits, etc. Also, be sure everyone at the party is "game" for this kind of game.

Sweat Suit Ballooon Stuff

You need: two oversized sweat suits to be worn by two children on each team. Plenty of "penny balloons" for everyone. Divide into two teams. Each team chooses someone to wear a sweat suit. At signal, each team attempts to "stuff" as many inflated balloons into the sweat

suit as possible within the given time limit (3 minutes is about right). Judge counts the balloons by popping them with a pin. Team with most balloons in the sweat suit wins.

For Food Ideas

Just about anything goes, but keep it simple, buffet style. Chocolate fondue recipes are available in fondue cookbooks. Or try an old-fashioned taffy pull:

Taffy to Pull

   ½ cup butter or margarine
   2 cups sugar
   1 cup molasses
 1½ cup water
   ¼ cup light corn syrup

Combine all ingredients in a large saucepan and cook over high heat, stirring until sugar is dissolved. Cook rapidly until mixture begins to thicken, then lower heat slightly and cook until a little of the mixture, dropped into cold water, forms a hard ball (260 degrees on a candy thermometer). Pour hot mixture onto a greased platter. When cool

enough to handle, butter hands lightly and pull candy until light in color and too hard to pull more. Stretch out into long rope 1½ inches in diameter. Cut into 1-inch pieces with scissors.

For Devotional Ideas

Use the following suggestions or improvise your own.

For example, perhaps you will want to eat later in the evening—around 11:00. Before you eat, form a circle and sing a song of praise. After snack time, have one of the children read Psalm 100. Then divide into teams and see who can write down the most "things to be thankful for" in two minutes.

Five minutes before midnight, everyone gathers together to listen to Psalm 150 (read by one of the dads). Then form one big circle, join hands and commit the new year to the Lord in prayer. (Let as many pray as want to.) At the stroke of 12, everyone grabs a noisemaker (pot, pan, spoon, etc.) and makes joyful family noise to praise the Lord and welcome the New Year.